COLLINS

HANDY ROAD ATLAS
BRITAIN
& IRELAND

CONTENTS

2 **Key to Map Symbols**
3-49 **Map Pages of Britain at 9 miles to 1 inch**
50-53 **Urban Area Maps at 4 miles to 1 inch**

50-51 London and M25

52-53 Birmingham

54-60 **Map Pages of Ireland at 16 miles to 1 inch**
61-77 **Index to Place Names in Britain**
78-79 **Index to Place Names in Ireland**

Collins Handy Road Atlas Britain and Ireland

Collins
An Imprint of HarperCollins*Publishers*
77–85 Fulham Palace Road, Hammersmith, London W6 8JB

© HarperCollins*Publishers* 1998

Printed in Hong Kong

ISBN 0 00 448615 3   BNL   KC9480

KEY TO SYMBOLS

ROAD INFORMATION

under constr.
M1

motorway

motorway tunnel

restricted access
1 ─────── 2

junction number

restricted access

service area

dual carriageway
A1

primary route

dual carriageway
A634 under constr.

'A' road

dual carriageway
B1246 under constr.

'B' road

other road

13

distance in miles

gradient

toll

OTHER TRANSPORT INFORMATION

railway

car ferry

✈ **airport**

CITIES, TOWNS AND VILLAGES

built-up areas

● ● ·

settlement

Scale: approx. 9 miles to 1 inch

0   10   20 miles

0   10   20   30 km

1 : 550 000

OTHER FEATURES

international boundary

national boundary

national / regional park

forest park

woodland

beach

marsh

canal

lake , dam and river

718
△

height in metres

TOURIST INFORMATION

☆

place of interest

feet		metres
2950		900
2295		700
1640		500
985		300
657		200
328		100
0		0
		land below sea level
		water

ADDITIONAL INFORMATION ON URBAN AREA MAPS PAGES 50-53

interchange

roundabout

Sta.

tourist railway

heliport

long distance path

m **ancient monument**

✕ **battle site**

⚑ **camping / caravanning**

castle

country park

❀ **garden**

golf course

historic house

historic house and garden

i **all year**   i **seasonal**
information centre

motor racing circuit

museum

nature reserve

race course

religious building

viewpoint

wildlife park

▲ **youth hostel**

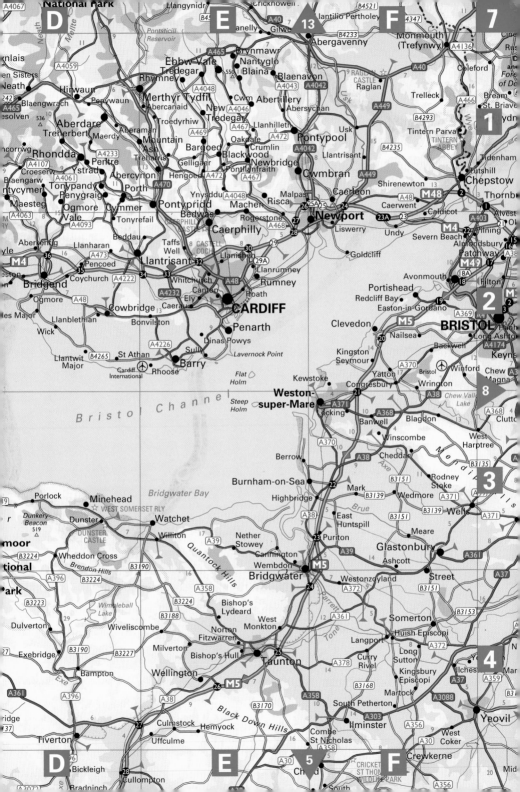

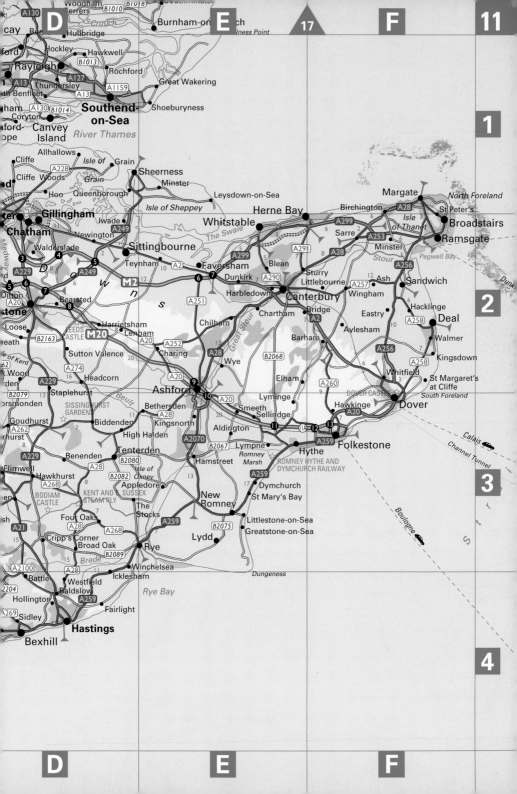

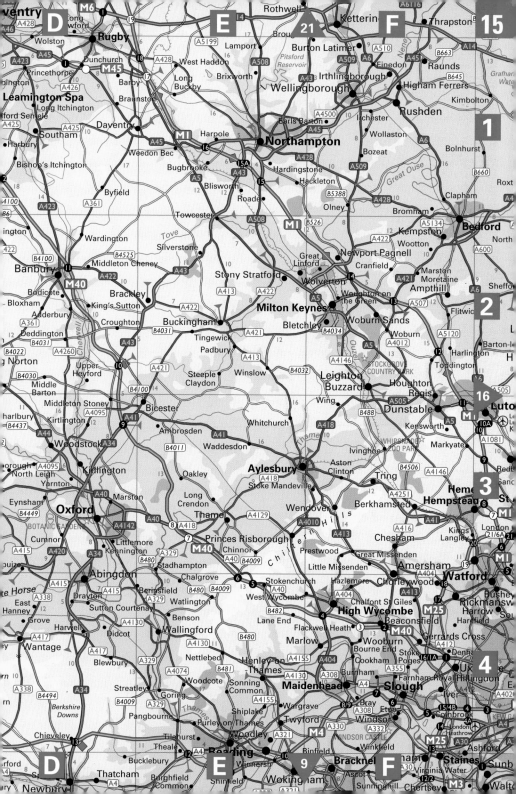

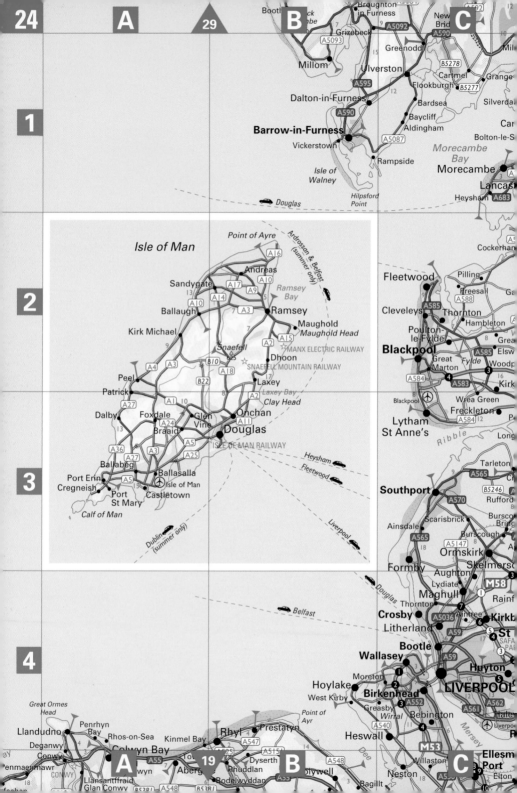

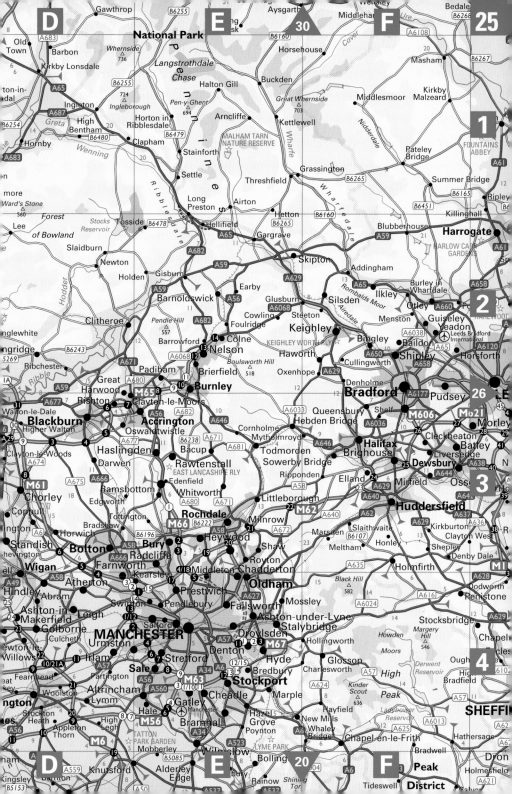

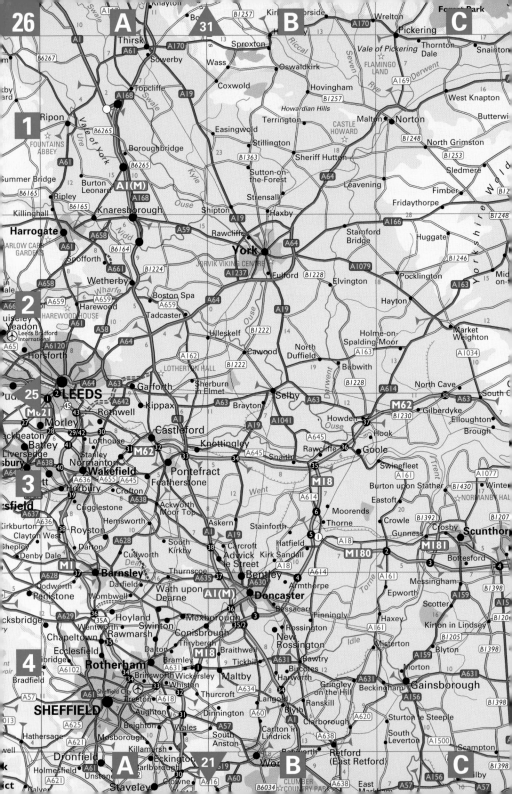

arborou
field
n
039
Filey
nby
10
d
vton
B1229   Bempton
A165
253
Flamborough Head
Flamborough
Rudston
SEWERBY HALL
Bridlington
Hilderthorpe
A614
12
A165

Driffield
Bridlington Bay

1249
Skipsea
Beeford
ick
15
B1242
sburton
B1244   Hornsea
Leven
Sigglesthorne
A1035
B1243
oft
A165
South Skirlaugh
rley
woodmansey
13
B1238
Aldbrough
Sproatley
Bilton
B1242
A1079
A165
Preston
Hedon
A1033
Withernsea
KINGSTON UPON HULL
A1033
Thorngumbald
B1362
63
Keyingham
A1033
21
Patrington
Humber
Goxhill
B1445
Barrow upon Humber
Easington
A1077
A160
Ulceby
5
Immingham
B1211
A180
8
Keelby
Healing
Humberside International
Grimsby
Cleethorpes
A46
6
A1084
A1173
Laceby
Humberston
13
Waltham
6
Caistor
A46
A18
A16
Tetney
434
17
North Thoresby
North Somercotes
03
B1225
B1203
Rotterdam and Zeebrugge
Binbrook
A1031
Fotherby
Market Rasen
15
A631
Grimoldby
B1200
Mablethorpe
B1202
A157
Louth
Manby
A157
B1399
A153
15
A1104
A52
A16
Maltby le Marsh
B1202
A111
22
ford
B1449
Tetford

Lincolnshire Wolds
Holderness
Mouth of The Humber
Spurn Head

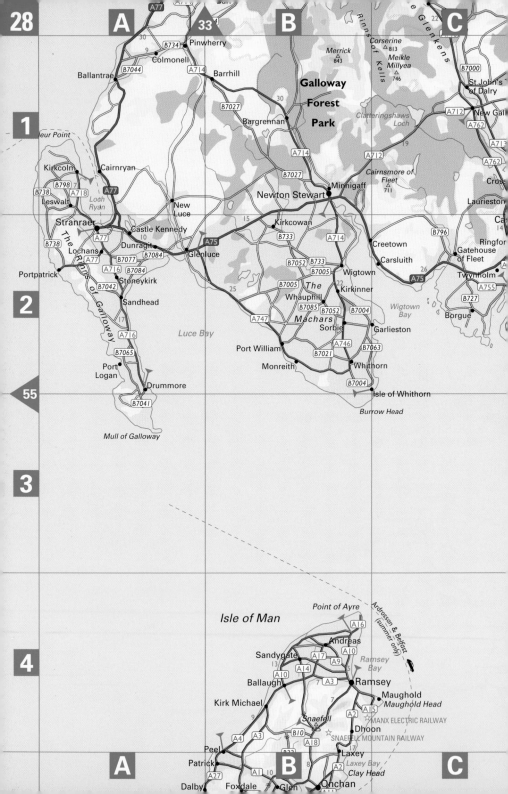

A77
B734 Pinwherry
Colmonell
B7044
Ballantrae
A714 Barrhill

Galloway

Forest

Park

Corserine 813
Merrick
843
Meikle
Millyea
746
Rinns of Kells
e Glenkens
B7000
St John's
of Dalry
A712 New Gal
A762
A712

Kirkcolm
B798 7
A718
Leswalt
B738
Cairnryan
A77
Loch
Ryan

1

Neur Point

B7027
Bargrennan

A714
B7027
Minnigaff
Clatteringshaws
Loch
A712
Cairnsmore of
Fleet
711
Laurieston
Ca
Cross

New
Luce
Newton Stewart

Stranraer
A77
Castle Kennedy
Dunragit
B7084
Glenluce
Lochans
A77
A716
B7077
Stoneykirk
B7042
Sandhead
The Rinns of Galloway
Portpatrick

A75
Kirkcowan
15
B733
A714
Creetown
Carsluith
A75
26
14
B796
Ringfor
Gatehouse
of Fleet
Twynholm
A755

B7052 B733
B7005
B7005
Wigtown
Kirkinner
Whauphill
B7085 B7052
Sorbie
22
25
A747
The
Machars
B7004
Garlieston
Borgue
Wigtown
Bay

2

Portpatrick
B738

A716
B7084

Luce Bay

Port William
Monreith
A746
B7021
B7063
Whithorn
B7004
Isle of Whithorn
Burrow Head

Port
Logan
B7065
Drummore
B7041
Mull of Galloway

55

3

Isle of Man

Point of Ayre
Ardrossan & Belfast
(summer only)

A16
Andreas
Sandygate
A17
A10
13
A14
A9
Ballaugh
A10
7
A3
Ramsey
Kirk Michael
7
Maughold
Maughold Head
A2
A15
Snaefell
Dhoon
MANX ELECTRIC RAILWAY
B10
A18
SNAEFELL MOUNTAIN RAILWAY
A4
A3
9
Peel
Laxey
Clay Head
A2
Laxey Bay
Patrick
A27
Dalby
Foxdale
10
Glen
Onchan
A1

Ramsey
Bay

4

Rum (Rhum)
Kinloch
Aird of Sloat
Point of S

Askival
812 △

Rubha nam
Meirleach

Cleadale

Eigg
An Sgurr
393 △
Galmisdale

Sound of Rum

Sound of Eigg

Sound of

1

Eilean
nan Each

Muck

Eilean
Shona
Ardtoe
Ockle
Ac
Achosnich
Point of
Ardnamurchan
Ardnamurchan
B8007
Ben Hiant
528 △
Kilchoan
Glenbeg
Glenborrodale

H
E
B
R
I
D
E
S

Eilean Mor
B8072
Sorisdale
Coll
Clabhach
B8071
Arinagour
Loch
Eatharna
B8070

Ardmore Point
Caliach
Point
Tobermory
B8073
Drimnin
Calgary
Dervaig
Loch
Frisa
Killundin
A848
Fi
B849
Kilninian

2

Gunna
Crossapol
Bay
Caolas
B8069
B8068
Tiree
B8065
Scarinish
Hough Bay
Hynish Bay
Barrapol
Balephuil
Balemartine

Calgary Bay
Loch Tuath
Treshnish Isles
Gometra
Ulva
Little
Colonsay
Staffa

Lagganulva
B8073
Salen
B8035
Knock
23
A849
Loch
Ba
Loch Na Keal
Balnahard
Ben More
966 △
Mull
B8035
Glen More
Ben Buie
717 △

3

I
N
N
E
R

IONA ABBEY
Iona
Fionnphort
Sound of Iona
Bunessan
Ross of Mull
Ardchiavaig

Loch Scridain
A849
35
Pennyghael
Carsaig
Malcolm's
Point
Loch Buie

Soa Island

4

Kiloran Bay
Rubh' a' Geodha
Colonsay
Kiloran
B8086
Scalasaig
Kilchattan
Loch Staosnaig
B8085
...arvard
nn Bhreac
467 △

Dubh Eilean
Oronsay
Shian Bay
Jura

Pabbay

Taobh
Tuath

A859

Loch
Langavat

An t-Òb

Sound of Pabbay

Boreray

Eilean
Bhearnaraigh

Roghadal

Renish Point

Port nan Long

Griminis Point

Vallay

Solas

A893

Sound of Harris

Baile Mhartainn

25

Uibhist a' Tuath
(North Uist)

A865

Ceann a'Bháigh

A865

A867

8

Loch na Madadh
(Lochmaddy)

Vaternish Point

Ben

Little Minch

Sound of Monach

Heisker or
Monach Islands

Baleshare

Saighdinis

Loch
Euphoirt

Dunvegan Head

Baile a'Mhanaich

Uachdar

Ronaigh
(Ronay)

Boreraig

Milovaig

Loch Dunvegan

Beinn na Faoghla
(Benbecula)

B892

Creag Ghoràidh

B891

B884

Ardivachar Point

Loch
Bee

Wiay

Bagh nam Faoilean

Healabhal
Bheag
△
488

A865

B890

Stadhlaigearraidh

Loch Sgioport

Uibhist a' Deas
(South Uist)

Rubha Ardvule

21

Beinn Mhor
△
620

Loch Eynor

A865

Dalabrog

Loch Baghasdail (Lochboisdale)

B888

Loch Baghasdail

Cille Bhrighde

Ludag

Sea of the Hebrides

Scurrival Point

Sound of Barra

Eiriosgaigh
(Eriskay)

Canna

Greian Head

Fuday

Eilean Barraigh
(Barra)

Borgh

A888

Earsàiridh

Bagh a' Chaisteil
(Castlebay)

Bhatarsaigh
(Vatersay)

Sanndraigh

Pabaigh

Miughalaigh
(Mingulay)

Bearnaraigh

Rubha Robhanais
Eoropaidh
Tabost
Dail Bho
Thuath
Port Nis
Sgiogarstaigh

A857
15

1

Muirneag
248
Tolastadh Úr
Tolsta Head

Arnol
Barabhas
Siabost
Bragar
West Loch Roag
A858
A857
Carlabhagh
20
Beinn
Mholach
292
Tolastadh
a'Chaolais
Breascleit
Great
Bernera
Griais
B895
Rubha an t-Siumpain
Port nan Giúran
Miabhig
Calanais
Stornoway
(Steornabhagh)
Newmarket
Tunga
Loch a'
Tuath
Timsgearraidh
Crulabhig
Gearraidh na h-Aibhne
A858
Siulaisiadar
An Rubha
A866
B8059
B8011
Loch
Suainaval
Achadh
Mór
A859
B897
Mealisval
574
Einacleit
B8011
13
2
reanais
12
Crosbost
Eilean Leodhais
Baile Ailein
Loch Erisort
sta
nd
(Lewis)
Loch
Langavat
B8060
Cearsiadar
Loch
Resort
21
Airidh
a'Bhruaich
Grabhair
Kebock Head
uisinis
Tirga Mor
679
A859
B8060
Leumrabhagh
Abhainnsuidhe
B887
Clishham
799
A859
Beinn
Mhór
572
Loch Seaforth
Loch Shell
Aird
Asaig
Loch
Claidh
The Minch
An Tairbeart
(Tarbert)
A859
3
Caolas Scalpaigh
Loch
Bhrollum
Sound of Taransay
25
*Eilean Scalpaigh
(Scalpay)*
East Loch Tarbert
Shiant Islands
**Ceann a Deas
na Hearadh
(South Harris)**
Rubha Rei
A859
Taobh
Tuath
Loch
Langavat
Melva
An t-Òb
Roghadal
Renish Point
of Harris

Rubha Hunish
Kilmaluag
4
end
A855
19
Balgown
Staffin Bay
Redpoin
Staffin
a Madadh
naddy)
Vaternish Point
Idrigil
Uig
Culnaknock
Fearnmore
Ben Geary
284
A8
40
Loch
Snizort
Trotternish
A855
13
Raasay
Dunvegan Head
Rona
Lusta

Little Minch

A   B   C

1

SHETLAND ISLES

Unst

Herma Ness

Norw
Valsgarth
Harolds
Baltasound

A968   10

Cullivoe
Belmont
Gutcher
Sellafirth

Uyeasound

Yell

Yell Sound

Point of
Fethaland

Isbister

A970

A968   18

Oddsta

Hascosay

Fetla

Houbie

B9088   Fu

Mid-Yell

The Faither

*Ronas
Hill*
450   Collafirth

A968   B9081

Otterswick

West Yell

Colgrave Sound

2

Ollaberry

Esha Ness
Stenness   B9078   Urafirth
Hillswick   A970

17

Ulsta   B9081   Hamnavoe
Burravoe

*St. Magnus
Bay*

Toft

B9076   10

A968

Brae

Out S

*Muckle
Roe*   Hillside
Voe   Laxo

Vidlin

Brough
Skaw   *Whalsay*

Isbister
Symbister

Dury Voe

*Papa
Stour*

B9071   *M*

B9071

A970   *a*

B9075

*South
Nesting Bay*

Sandness   A971   *l*

Aith   B9075

Bixter   Setter   20

3

Bridge
of Walls   Heglibister

Girlsta

Walls   B9071

Garderhouse

Culswick

Veensgarth

B9074   Lerwick

*Isle of
Ness*

Scalloway   *a*

Bressay

Hamnavoe   B9074

Easter
Quarff

Bergen (summer only)

Ham   *West
Burra*

Foula   A970

Cunningsburgh

25   Sandwick

Mousa

4

B9122   Levenwick

Scousburgh   A970

Boddam

Toab   Grutness

urgh   *Sumburgh
Head*

A   B   C

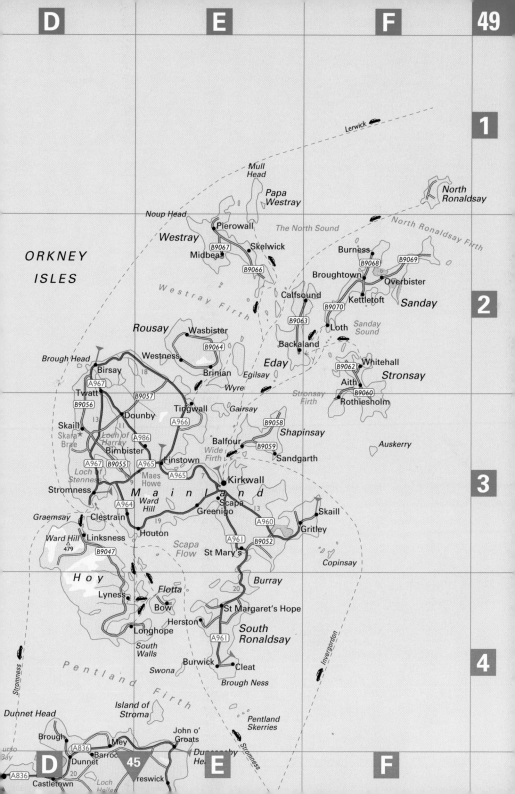

Scale: 1 2 3 4 5 miles / 1 2 3 4 5 6 7 8 km

Grid columns: E F G H

Grid rows: 1 2 3 4 5

Places visible on map (selection):

HODDESDON, Broxbourne, Hammond Street, Churchgate, CHESHUNT, Waltham Abbey, ENFIELD, Ponders End, Edmonton, Tottenham, WALTHAM FOREST, Walthamstow, Wanstead, Stoke Newington, Leyton, HACKNEY, Tower Hamlets, Stepney, NEWHAM, City of London, Bermondsey, GREENWICH, SOUTHWARK, LEWISHAM, Dulwich, Sydenham, Crystal Palace, Penge, Beckenham, BROMLEY, CROYDON, Shirley, New Addington, Selsdon, Sanderstead, Warlingham, Whyteleafe, Woldingham, Tatsfield

Great Parndon, Roydon, Lower Nazeing, Nazeing, Wormley, Turnford, Upshire, Epping, Theydon Bois, Loughton, High Beach, Buckhurst Hill, Chingford, CHIGWELL, Woodford Green, Grange Hill, Hainault, Woodford Bridge, REDBRIDGE, Seven Kings, Ilford, Becontree, BARKING & DAGENHAM, Barking, East Ham, Beckton, Creekmouth, Thamesmead, Abbey Wood, Woolwich, Plumstead, Belvedere, Charlton, Shooter's Hill, East Wickham, Welling, Kidbrooke, Eltham, BEXLEY, Bexleyheath, New Eltham, Sidcup, Foots Cray, Chislehurst, Bickley, St Paul's Cray, Orpington, Locksbottom, Farnborough, Green Street Green, Chelsfield, Pratt's Bottom, Knockholt, Halstead, Biggin Hill, Cudham, Downe, Keston, West Wickham, Hayes, Eden Park, Addington

Threshers Bush, Foster Street, Magdalen Laver, Hastingwood, North Weald Bassett, Epping Green, Epping Upland, Thornwood Common, Coppersale Common, Toot Hill, Fiddlers Hamlet, Stanford Rivers, Stapleford Tawney, Passingford Bridge, Abridge, Lambourne End, Stapleford Abbotts, Navestock, Noak Hill, Havering-atte-Bower, Harold Hill, Collier Row, Gidea Park, Romford, Rush Green, Hornchurch, Upminster, HAVERING, Cranham, Elm Park, Dagenham, South Hornchurch, Rainham, Wennington, Aveley, North Ockendon, South Ockendon, Purfleet, West Thurrock, Grays

Moreton, Bobbingworth, Shelley, Fyfield, Chipping Ongar, High Ongar, Norton Mandeville, Norton Heath, Blackmore, Stondon Massey, Kelvedon Hatch, Doddinghurst, Mountnessing, Navestock Side, Coxtie Green, South Weald, BRENTWOOD, Great Warley, Little Warley, Childerditch, Herongate, Ingrave, East Horndon, West Horndon, Bulphan, Orsett, Baker Street, Chadwell St Mary, Tilbury, Northfleet, GRAVESEND, Swanscombe, Greenhithe, Dartford, Crayford, Hextable, Swanley, Crockenhall, Eynsford, Farningham, Horton Kirby, Sutton at Hone, South Darenth, Darenth, Hook Green, Longfield, New Barn, Hartley, Fawkham Green, West Kingsdown, Ash, Stansted, Fairseat, Wrotham, Kemsing, Otford, Borough Green, Kingsdown, Ightham

Berners Roding, Shellow Bowells, Willingale, Great Oxney Green, Cooksmill Green, Heybridge, Ingatestone, Hutton, Shenfield, Tye Common, Little Burstead, Dunton Wayletts, Laindon, Langdon Hills, Horndon on the Hill, Stanford-le-Hope, Mucking, Chadwell St Mary, Meopham, Sole Street, Camer, Vigo Village, Culverstone Green, Harvel, Trottiscliffe, Stansted

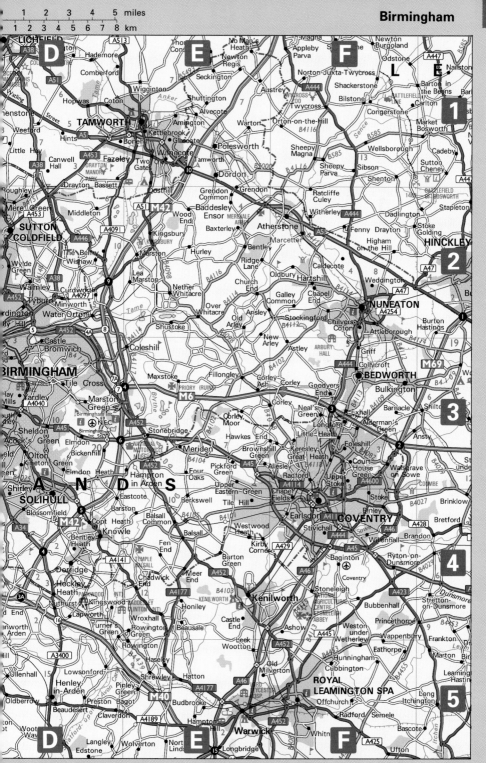

A **B** **C**

Scale: approx. 16 miles to 1 inch

| 0 | 10 | 20 | 30 | 40 miles |
| 0 | 10 | 20 | 30 | 40 | 50 | 60 km |

1 : 978 000

Malin
Ba

Dunaff
Head

Tory Island

Horn
Head

Fanad Head

Portsalon

Dr

Tory Sound

Sheep
Haven

Lough
Swilly

Inishbofin

Ards
Forest Park

Mulray
Bay

R246

R246

R24

Bloody Foreland

R257

Muckish
Mountain

Creeslough

Milford

Isla

Gweedore

Gortahork

Glenveagh
National
Park

Lough
Keel

Lough
Fen

Gola Island

Bunbeg

Gweedore

N56

Owey Island

R257

Errigal

R251

Kilmacrenan

R255

R249

Rosses Bay

Nacung
L.

Slieve
Snaght

Beagh

Lough
Gartan

N56

R245

The Rosses

Anure
Lough

Derryveagh Mts

R254

R251

Letterkenny

R250

Burtonport

N56

Swilly

Aran Island

R259

Dunglee

Cronamuck
Mountain

Cark
Mountain

R250

Raphoe

N13

R236

Liffor

Crohy Head

R252

Croagheheen

Fintown

R252

Deele

Stranorlar

Gweebarra Bay

R250

Lough
Finn

Blue Stack Mts

Lough Mourne

N15

Clady

Dawros Head

Aghla
Mountain

18

R235

Loughros More
Bay

R261

Glenties

R262

Blue
Stack

Castlederg

Glen
Bay

Ardara

Slievetooey

Glengesh Pass

Lough
Eske

N15

Derg

B72

Rossan Point

Malin Bay

Malin More

Crownarad

Donegal

B5C

Rathlin O'Birne Island

R263

Slieve
League

Killybegs

N56

R232

Pettigo

B4

Muckross Head

Fintragh Bay

McSwynes Bay

Inver Bay

Doorin
Point

13

R231

Boa Island

B136

Lisnarrick

Dro

A32

St John's
Point

Ballyshannon

Erne

Lough
Erne

Tully

Enn

Donegal Bay

R279

Bundoran

N3

B52

Lough Melvin

B82

B123

Mullaghmore
Head

4

Tullybrack

A46

Inishmurray

Cliffonoy

23

R281

B52

B81

Broad Haven

Streedagh Point

N15

Darty Mts

Glenade
Lough

Lough
Macnean Upper

Belcoo

Enni

Downpatrick
Head

Roskeeragh Point

Benbulben

Truskmore

Glencar
Lake

Dough
Mt

R282

R281

B52

A32

A4

Belderg

Lenadoon
Point

Sligo
Bay

Drumcliff

R291

N16

Florence Court
Forest Park

B108

Maumakeogh

Ballycastle

Killala
Bay

Aughris
Head

Coney
I.

Sligo

Manorhamilton

Glengavlen

Cuncagh

B51

R314

Bartragh

R297

R286

R286

R280

Belhavel
Lough

Slievenakilla

Bellavally
Gap

New
Slieve
Rushen

Killala

R315

R314

Dromore
West

N59

Knockalonga

Colloney

R292

N4

R287

R287

Drumkeeran

R200

R207

Iron Mountains

N87

Slieve Gamph

24

R293

R288

R289

R280

Bencroy

Ballyconnell

R205

Ballina

R294

Easky
Lough

N17

Ballymote

Lough
Arrow

R284

Lough
Allen

Slieve Anierin

Ballinamore

Lou
Ough

R312

R316

R315

R310

Mullany's Cross

N26

Templehouse
Lake

R296

Ballinafad

R295

Lough
Key

Lough Key
Forest Park

R284

R280

Killykeen
Forest Pa

R201

Nephin
Beg Range

Lough
Levally
Lough

Foxford

20

Tubbercurry

R293

R294

Boyle

R209

R202

Carriga

Beltra
Lough

Pontoon

N26

7

Charlestown

R294

Cavetown
Lough

Carrick-on-Shannon

R203

Birreencorragh

R312

Swinford

N5

Ballaghaderreen

R361

Drumharlow
Lough

32

Mohill

Lough
Feeagh

R311

R310

Bohola

R320

Urlaur
Lough

N5

Frenchpark

R368

Bofin
Lough

N4

Rinn
Lough

R202

Dromod

R198

Newport

N59

Islandeady
Lough

Castlebar

Kiltimagh

N83

R323

R293

R361

R369

R368

R371

Clooneagh

Lough
Gowna

Arv

Croagh
Patrick

N5

N84

Knock

Ballyhaunis

rea

N17

N61

Tulsk

Strokestown

Longford

Kilglass
Lough

R194

R330

R320

Foxford

Ros

Rathlin O'Birne

1

2

3

4

Stags of Broad Haven

Benwee Head

Erris Head

Downpatrick Head

Lenadoor Point

Broad Haven

Belderg

Ballycastle

Killala Bay

R297

Belmullet

R314

Maumakeogh

R314

Bartragh

Killala

N59

Glenamoy

Carrowmore Lake

The Mullet

R313

R313

Bangor Erris

R315

R314

L

Inishkea North

N59

Owenmore

Lough Dahybaun

Ballina

R294

Inishkea South

Owenmore

Mullany's Cre

Duvillaun More

Blacksod Bay

Ballycroy

Slieve Car

Deel

Nephin Beg

R312

R316

R315

Nephin

R310

Foxford

N26

Croaghaun

Slieve More

Dooagh

Annagh

Owenduff

Birreencorragh

Levally Lough

Lough Conn

N26 E

Swinford

Achill Head

Nephin Beg Range

Cushcamcarragh

Pontoon

N58

R321

Bohola

Achill Island

R319

Achill

Lough Feeagh

R317

Beltra Lough

N5

R320

Corraun Peninsula

Mulrany

R312

R310

Castlebar

R320

Achillbeg Island

Newport

R311

Islandeady Lough

Kiltimagh

R3

Clare Island

Clew Bay

N59

Westport

N5

11

Knock

R323

R324

Louisburgh

R335

Croagh Patrick

R330

N60

R320

Murrisk

N84

Partry

Claremorris

Ba

Caher Island

Cregganbaun

R335

Partry Mts

R331

Inishturk

Benbury

Bengorm

Benwee

Lough Mask

18

Inishbofin

Mweelrea

Aasleagh

Devils Mother

Ballinrobe

R334

R332

Inishark

Ballynakill Bay

Lough Fee

R336

Joyce's Country

Kilmaine

Omey Island

Connemara National Park

N59

Benbaun

R334

Benbaun

R345

Cong

N84

Clifden

The Twelve Pins

Bencorr

Lough Inagh

R336

R334

R333

Mannin Bay

Connemara

Recess

Lough Corrib

Headford

Slyne Head

R342 R340

R336

R341

Bertraghboy Bay

Ballyconneely Bay

Iar Connaght

N84

R340

Glenicmurrin Lough

N59

Owenboliska

N17 N1

Mweenish Island

R343

Galway

N6

Gorumna Island

R336

Tawin Island

Kilcolga

Golam Head

Black Head

Eddy Island

North Sound

Murroogh

N67

Inismore

Ballyvaughan

Aran Islands

Inishmaan

Inisheer

R477

Slieve Elva

Burren

South Sound

R479

R480

Lisdoonvarna

Doolin Point

R481

R476

R460

Cliffs of Moher

R478

Lickeen Lough

R476

Ennistymon Inch

Corofin

Lough Atedau

N67

R460

Auchencairn 29 D2
Auchencrow 35 E2
Auchindrain 37 E4
Auchinleck 33 F3
Auchmull 39 E1
Auchnagatt 43 F3
Aucholzie 39 D1
Auchterarder 38 B4
Auchtermuchty 39 D4
Auchtertool 34 B1
Audlem 20 A2
Audley 20 A2
Aughton Lancs. 24 C4
Aughton S.Yorks. 26 A4
Auldearn 42 B2
Aultbea 41 D1
Aultguish Inn 41 E2
Austrey 53 E1
Aveley 10 C1
Aveley 51 G3
Aviemore 42 B4
Avoch 42 A2
Avonbridge 34 A1
Avonmouth 7 F2
Awre 14 A3
Awsworth 21 D2
Axminster 5 F1
Aycliffe 31 D3
Aylesbury 15 E3
Aylesford 11 D2
Aylesham 11 F2
Aylsham 23 E3
Ayr 33 E3
Aysgarth 30 C4

B

Babworth 26 B4
Backaland 49 E2
Backwell 7 F2
Bacup 25 E3
Badcaul 44 A4
Baddesley Ensor 53 E2
Badenscoth 43 E3
Badgers Mount 51 F5
Badlipster 45 F2
Badsey 14 B2
Bagh a' Chaisteil
    (Castlebay) 46 A4
Bagillt 19 E1
Baginton 53 F4
Baglan 6 C1
Bagshot 9 F1
Baildon 25 F2
Baile Ailein 47 E2
Baile a'Mhanaich 46 A2
Baile Mhartainn 46 A1
Bainbridge 30 B4
Bainton 26 C2
Baker Street 51 H3
Bala 19 D3
Balbeggie 38 C3
Balblair 42 A2
Balcombe 10 B3
Balderton 21 E2
Baldslow 11 D4
Balemartine 36 A3
Balephuil 36 A3
Balfour 49 E3
Balfron 33 F1
Balgown 40 B2
Balgray 39 D3
Balintore 42 A2
Ballabeg 24 A3
Ballachulish 37 E2
Ballantrae 28 A1

Ballasalla 24 A3
Ballater 39 D1
Ballaugh 24 A2
Ballingry 38 C4
Ballinluig 38 C2
Ballintuim 38 C2
Balloch 33 E1
Ballochroy 32 C2
Ballygrant 32 A2
Balmacara 40 C3
Balmaha 33 E1
Balmedie 43 F4
Balnacra 41 D3
Balnahard 36 C3
Balnapaling 42 A2
Balquhidder 38 A3
Balsall 53 E4
Balsall Common 53 E4
Baltasound 48 C1
Balvicar 37 D4
Bamburgh 35 F3
Bampton Devon 7 D4
Bampton Oxon. 14 C3
Banbury 15 D2
Banchory 39 E1
Banff 43 E2
Bangor 18 B1
Banham 23 D4
Bankfoot 38 C3
Bannockburn 34 A1
Banstead 10 B2
Banwell 7 F3
Bar Hill 16 B1
Barabhas 47 E1
Barassie 33 E3
Barbaraville 42 A2
Barbon 25 D1
Barby 15 D1
Bardney 22 A1
Bardsea 24 C1
Bargoed 7 E1
Bargrennan 28 B1
Barham 11 F2
Barking Gt.Lon. 51 F3
**Barking & Dagenham
    51 F3**
Barkingside 51 F3
Barkston 21 F2
Barkway 16 B2
Barlaston 20 B2
Barlborough 21 D1
Barley 16 B2
Barmouth 12 C1
Barnacle 53 F3
Barnard Castle 30 C3
Barnes 50 D4
Barnet 50 D2
Barningham 17 D1
Barnoldswick 25 E2
Barnsley 26 A4
Barnstaple 6 C4
Barnt Green 52 C4
Barnton 20 A1
Barr 33 E4
Barrapol 36 A3
Barrhead 33 F2
Barrhill 28 B1
Barrock 45 F1
Barrow upon Humber
    27 D3
Barrow upon Soar 21 E3
Barrow-in-Furness 24 B1
Barrowford 25 E2
Barry 7 E2
Barston 53 E4
Barton (Preston) Lancs.
    25 D2

Barton in the Beans
    53 F1
Barton-le-Clay 16 A3
Barton-under-Needwood
    20 C3
Barton-upon-Humber
    27 D3
Baschurch 19 F3
Basildon 11 D1
Basingstoke 9 E1
Baslow 20 C1
Bassingham 21 F1
Batchworth 50 B2
Batchworth Heath 50 B2
Bath 8 B1
Batheaston 8 B1
Bathford 8 B1
Bathgate 34 A1
Batley 25 F3
Battersea 50 D4
Battle 11 D4
Bawdeswell 23 D3
Bawdsey 17 E2
Bawtry 26 B4
Baxterley 53 E2
Baycliff 24 C1
Bayford Herts. 51 E1
Bayston Hill 13 F1
Beaconsfield 10 A1
Beadnell 35 F3
Beaminster 5 F1
Bean 51 G4
Bearsden 33 F1
Bearsted 11 D2
Beattock 34 B4
**Beauchamp Roding
    51 G1**
Beaudesert 53 D5
Beauly 41 F3
Beaumaris 18 B1
Beausale 53 E4
Bebington 19 E1
Beccles 23 F4
Beckenham 51 E5
Beckingham 26 C4
Beckton 51 F3
Becontree 51 F3
Bedale 31 D4
Beddau 7 D2
Beddgelert 18 B2
Beddingham 10 C4
Beddington 51 E5
Beddington Corner 50 D5
Bedford 15 F2
Bedlington 30 C1
Bedmond 50 C1
Bedwas 7 E2
Bedworth 21 D4
Bedworth 53 F3
Beeford 27 D2
Beer 5 E1
Beeston Notts. 21 D2
Beighton S.Yorks. 26 A4
Beith 33 E2
Belbroughton 20 B4
Belbroughton 52 B4
Belford 35 F3
Bell Bar 50 D1
Bell End 52 B4
Bellingdon 50 A1
Bellingham 30 B1
Bellshill N.Lan. 33 F2
Belmont Gt.Lon. **50 D5**
Belmont Shet. 48 C1
Belper 21 D2
Belsay 30 C1

Belvedere 51 F4
Bembridge 9 E4
Bempton 27 D1
Benenden 11 D3
Benllech 18 B1
Benson 15 E4
Bentley S.Yorks. 26 B4
Bentley Warks. 53 E2
Bentley Heath 53 D4
Beoley 52 C5
Bere Alston 4 B2
Bere Ferrers 4 B2
Bere Regis 8 B3
Berinsfield 15 D4
Berkeley 14 A3
Berkhamsted 15 F3
Berkhamsted 50 A1
Berkswell 20 C4
Berkswell 53 E4
Bermondsey 51 E4
Berners Roding 51 H1
Bernisdale 40 B2
Berriedale 45 E3
Berrow 7 E3
Bersham 19 E2
Berwick-upon-Tweed
    35 E2
Bessacarr 26 B4
Bethersden 11 E3
Bethesda 18 B2
Bethnal Green 51 E3
Betsham 51 H4
Bettyhill 44 C1
Betws-y-coed 18 C2
Beverley 27 D2
Bewdley 20 A4
Bexhill 11 D4
Bexley 51 F4
Bexleyheath 51 F4
Bibury 14 C3
Bicester 15 E3
Bickenhill 53 D3
Bickleigh (Plymouth) Devon
    4 C2
Bickleigh (Tiverton) Devon
    5 D1
Bickley 51 F5
Bicknacre 16 C4
Biddenden 11 D3
Biddulph 20 B1
Bideford 6 B4
Bidford-on-Avon 14 C1
Bigbury-on-Sea 4 C3
Biggar 34 A3
Biggin Hill 10 C2
Biggleswade 16 A2
Bilbrook Staffs. 52 A1
Bilbster 45 F2
Billericay 11 C4
Billinge 25 D4
Billingham 31 D3
Billinghay 22 A2
Billingshurst 10 A3
Billockby 23 F3
Billy Row 30 C2
Bilston Midloth. 34 B2
Bilston W.Mid. 52 B2
Bilstone 53 F1
Bilton 27 D3
Bimbister 49 E3
Binbrook 27 D4
Binfield 9 F1
Bingham 21 E2
Bingley 25 F2
Binley W.Mid. 53 F4
Birchgrove N.P.T.
    6 C1

Birchington 11 F1
Bircotes 26 B4
Bird End 52 C2
Birkenhead 19 E1
Birmingham 20 C4
Birmingham 52 C3
Birmingham International
    Airport 20 C4
**Birmingham International
    Airport 53 D3**
Birsay 49 D3
Birstall 21 E3
Birtley T. & W. 31 D2
Bishop Auckland 30 C3
Bishopbriggs 33 F1
Bishop's Castle 13 F2
Bishop's Cleeve 14 B2
Bishop's Hull 7 E4
Bishop's Itchington 15 D1
Bishop's Lydeard 7 E4
Bishop's Stortford 16 B3
Bishop's Tawton 6 C4
Bishop's Waltham 9 E3
Bishop's Wood 52 A1
Bishopston 6 C1
Bishopton Renf. 33 F1
Bisley 14 B3
Bitton 8 A1
Bixter 48 B3
Blaby 21 D4
Black Bourton 14 C3
Black Notley 16 C3
Blackburn Aber. 43 E4
Blackburn Lancs. 25 D3
Blackburn W.Loth. 34 A2
Blackford 38 B4
Blackhall Colliery 31 D2
Blackheath W.Mid. 52 B3
Blacklunans 38 C2
Blackmoor Gate 6 C3
Blackmore 51 H1
Blackpool 24 C2
Blackpool Airport 24 C3
Blackridge 34 A1
Blackwaterfoot 32 C3
Blackwell H. & W. 52 B4
Blackwood 7 E1
Blaenau Ffestiniog 18 C2
Blaenavon 7 E1
Blaengarw 7 D1
Blaengwrach 7 D1
Blagdon 7 F3
Blaich 37 E1
Blaina 7 E1
Blair Atholl 38 B2
Blairgowrie 38 C3
Blakebrook 52 A4
Blakedown 52 A4
Blakeney Glos. 14 A3
Blakeney Norf. 23 D2
Blakenhall W.Mid. 52 B2
Blakeshall 52 A4
Blandford Forum 8 B3
Blaydon 30 C1
Blean 11 E2
Bletchley 15 F2
Blewbury 15 D4
Blisworth 15 E1
Blockley 14 C2
Blossomfield 53 D4
Bloxham 15 D2
Bloxwich 52 B1
Blubberhouses 25 F2
Blyth Nhumb. 31 D1
Blyth Notts. 26 B4
Blyth Bridge 34 B2
Blyton 26 C4

at of Garten 42 B4
ath 41 F2
bbington 52 A2
bbingworth 51 G1
ddam *Aber.* 43 F3
ddam *Shet.* 48 B4
delwyddan 19 D1
denham 13 F3
dicote 15 D2
dmin 4 A2
gniebrae 43 D3
gnor Regis 9 F3
Idon 31 D2
Idre 9 D3
Ilington (Macclesfield)
   Ches. 20 B1
Inhurst 16 A1
Isover 21 D1
Itby 31 D4
Iton *E.Loth.* 34 C1
Iton *Gt.Man.* 25 D3
Iton-le-Sands 24 C1
Iventor 4 A2
nar Bridge 44 C4
nawe 37 E3
nawe Quarries 37 E3
nchester Bridge 35 D4
nehill 53 D1
'ness 34 A1
ningale 52 A1
njedward 35 D3
nnybridge 34 A1
nnyrigg 34 C2
nvilston 7 E2
otle *Cumb.* 29 E4
otle *Mersey.* 19 E1
reham 16 C3
rehamwood 16 A4
rehamwood 50 C2
reland 34 B4
reraig 40 A2
rgh 46 A4
rgue *D. & G.* 28 C2
rgue *High.* 45 E3
rough Green 10 C2
roughbridge 26 A1
rrowash 21 D2
rrowdale 29 F3
rth 12 C2
rve 40 B3
sbury 14 A2
scastle 4 A1
sham 9 F3
ston 22 A2
ston Spa 26 A2
tany Bay **50 D2**
tesdale 17 D1
thel 29 E2
thenhampton 5 F1
tley *Bucks.* 50 A1
ttesford *Leics.* 21 E2
ttesford *N.Lincs.* 26 C3
ughton 21 E1
urnbrook 52 C3
urne 22 A3
urne End *Bucks.* 15 F4
urne End *Herts.* 50 B1
urnebridge 51 G2
urnemouth 8 C3
urnemouth Airport 8 C3
urnheath 52 B4
urnmoor 31 D2
urnville 52 C3
urton 8 B2
urton-on-the-Water
   14 C3
veney 50 A4

Bovey Tracey 5 D2
Bovingdon 50 B1
Bovinger 51 G1
Bow 49 E4
Bowburn 31 D2
Bowes 30 B3
Bowmore 32 A2
Bowness-on-Solway 29 E1
Bowness-on-Windermere
   29 F4
Box 8 B1
Boxmoor 50 B1
Boyton Cross 51 H1
Bozeat 15 F1
Braaid 24 A3
Bracadale 40 A3
Bracebridge Heath 21 F1
Brackley 15 E2
Bracknell 9 F1
Braco 38 B4
Bracora 37 D1
Bradford *W.Yorks.* 25 F2
Bradford-on-Avon 8 B1
Brading 9 E4
Bradley *W.Mid.* 52 B2
Bradmore *W.Mid.* 52 A2
Bradninch 5 E1
Bradpole 5 F1
Bradshaw 25 D3
Bradwell *Derbys.* 25 F4
Bradwell *Norf.* 23 F4
Bradwell Waterside 17 D3
Brae 48 B2
Braeantra 41 F1
Braemar 38 C1
Bragar 47 E1
Brailsford 20 C2
Braintree 16 C3
Braithwaite 29 E3
Braithwell 26 B4
Bramford 17 E2
Bramhall 25 E4
Bramley *S.Yorks.* 26 A4
Brampton *Cambs.* 16 A1
Brampton *Cumb.* 30 A2
Brampton *Suff.* 17 F1
Brancaster 22 C2
Brandesburton 27 D2
Brandon *Dur.* 30 C2
Brandon *Suff.* 22 C4
Branson's Cross 52 C4
Branston 21 F1
Brantham 17 E2
Bratton 8 B1
Braunston 15 D1
Braunstone 21 D3
Braunton 6 B4
Bray 10 A1
Brayton 26 B3
Breage 3 E3
Breakish 40 C4
Bream 14 A3
Breanais 47 D2
Breascleit 47 E2
Breaston 21 D2
Brechfa 12 B4
Brechin 39 E2
Brecon 13 D4
Bredbury 25 E4
Bredon 14 B2
Brent 50 C3
Brentford 50 C4
Brentwood 10 C1
Brentwood 51 G2
Bretton 19 E2
Brewood 20 B3
Brewood 52 A1

Bricket Wood 50 C1
Bridge 11 E2
Bridge of Allan 38 B4
Bridge of Balgie 38 A2
Bridge of Cally 38 C2
Bridge of Craigisla 39 D2
Bridge of Don 43 F4
Bridge of Dun 39 E2
Bridge of Dye 39 E1
Bridge of Earn 38 C4
Bridge of Orchy 37 F3
Bridge of Walls 48 B3
Bridge of Weir 33 E2
Bridgend *Angus* 39 E2
Bridgend *Bridgend* 7 D2
Bridgend *Moray* 42 C3
Bridgend (Islay) *Arg. & B.*
   32 A2
Bridgend (Lochgilphead)
   Arg. & B. 32 C1
Bridgnorth 20 A4
Bridgtown 52 B1
Bridgwater 7 E4
Bridlington 27 D1
Bridport 5 F1
Brierfield 25 E3
Brierley Hill 52 B3
Brig o'Turk 38 A4
Brigg 26 C3
Brigham 29 E3
Brighouse 25 F3
Brighstone 9 D4
Brightlingsea 17 D3
Brighton 10 B4
Brigstock 21 F4
Brimington 21 D1
Brinian 49 E2
Brinsley 21 D2
Brinsworth 26 A4
Bristol 14 A4
Bristol Airport 8 A1
Briston 23 D3
Briton Ferry 6 C1
Brixham 5 D3
Brixworth 15 E1
Broad Haven 12 A2
Broad Heath 14 A1
Broad Oak 11 D3
Broadclyst 5 D1
Broadford 40 C4
Broadley Common 51 F1
Broadmayne 8 B4
Broadstairs 11 F2
Broadway 14 C2
Broadwey 8 A4
Broadwindsor 5 F1
Brochel 40 B3
Brockenhurst 9 D3
Brockworth 14 B3
Brodick 33 D3
Bromham *Beds.* 15 F1
Bromham *Wilts.* 8 C1
Bromley F5
Brompton 31 D4
Brompton on Swale 30 C4
Bromsgrove 14 B1
Bromsgrove 52 B4
Bromyard 14 A1
Bronaber 18 C2
Brook Street *Essex* 51 G2
Brooke 23 E4
Brookmans Park 16 A4
Brookmans Park 50 D1
Broome *H. & W.* 52 B4
Broomfield 16 C3
Brora 45 D4
Broseley 20 A4

Brotton 31 E3
Brough *Cumb.* 30 B3
Brough *E.Riding* 26 C3
Brough *High.* 45 E1
Brough *Shet.* 48 C2
Broughton *Flints.* 19 E2
Broughton *N.Lincs.* 26 C3
Broughton *Northants.*
   21 F4
Broughton *Sc.Bord.* 34 B3
Broughton Astley 21 D4
Broughton in Furness
   29 E4
Broughtown 49 F2
Broughty Ferry 39 E3
Brownhills *W.Mid.* 20 B3
Brownhills *W.Mid.* 52 C1
Brownshill Green 53 F3
Broxbourne 51 F1
Broxburn 34 B1
Brundall 23 E3
Brundish 17 E1
Bruton 8 A2
Brynamman 6 C1
Brynford 19 E1
Brynmawr 7 E1
Bubbenhall 53 F4
Bubwith 26 B2
Buchlyvie 33 F1
Buckden *Cambs.* 16 A1
Buckden *N.Yorks.* 25 E1
Buckfastleigh 4 C2
Buckhaven 39 D4
Buckhurst Hill 51 F2
Buckie 43 D2
Buckingham 15 E2
Buckland Common 50 A1
Bucklebury 9 E1
Buckley 19 E2
Bucks Hill 50 B1
Bucksburn 43 E4
Budbrooke 53 E5
Bude 4 A1
Budleigh Salterton 5 E2
Bugbrooke 15 E1
Builth Wells 13 D3
Buldoo 45 E1
Bulford 8 C2
Bulkington *Warks.* 21 D4
Bulkington *Warks.* 53 F3
Bulmer Tye 17 D2
Bulphan S1 H3
Bumble's Green 51 F1
Bunessan 36 B3
Bungay 23 E4
Buntingford 16 B3
Burbage 9 D1
Bures 17 D2
Burford 14 C3
Burgess Hill 10 B3
Burgh by Sands 29 F2
Burgh le Marsh 22 B1
Burghead 42 B2
Burghfield Common 9 E1
Burghill 13 F3
Burley 9 D3
Burley in Wharfdale 25 F2
Burness 49 F2
Burnham *Bucks.* 10 A1
Burnham *Bucks.* 50 A3
Burnham Market 22 C2
Burnham-on-Crouch 17 D4
Burnham-on-Sea 7 E3
Burnhouse 33 E2
Burniston 31 F4
Burnley 25 E2
Burnmouth 35 E2

Burnopfield 30 C2
Burntisland 34 B1
Burntwood Green 20 C3
Burntwood Green 52 C1
Burravoe 48 C2
Burrelton 38 C3
Burrowhill 50 A5
Burry Port 6 B1
Burscough 24 C3
Burscough Bridge 24 C3
Bursledon 9 E3
Burton Bradstock 5 F1
**Burton Green *Warks.*
   53 E4**
Burton Joyce 21 E2
Burton Latimer 15 F1
Burton Leonard 26 A1
Burton upon Stather 26 C3
Burton upon Trent 20 C3
Burton-in-Kendal 25 D1
Burwardsley 19 F2
Burwarton 20 A4
Burwash 11 D3
Burwell 16 B1
Burwick 49 E4
Bury 25 E3
Bury St. Edmunds 17 D1
Bushbury 52 B1
Bushey 16 A4
Bushey 50 C2
Bushey Heath 50 C2
Buttermere 29 E3
Butterwick 26 C1
Buxted 10 C3
Buxton 20 B1
Byfield 15 D1
Byfleet 10 A2
Byfleet 50 B5
Bylchau 19 D2

C

Caerau *Cardiff* 7 E2
Caergwrle 19 E2
Caerhun 18 C1
Caerleon 7 F1
Caernarfon 18 B2
Caerphilly 7 E2
Caerwent 7 F1
Cairnbaan 32 C1
Cairndow 37 E4
Cairneyhill 34 A1
Cairnryan 28 A1
Caister-on-Sea 23 F3
Caistor 27 D4
Calanais 47 E2
Caldbeck 29 F2
Caldecote *Warks.* 53 F2
Caldecott 21 F4
Caldercruix 34 A1
Caldicot 7 F2
Caldwell 30 C3
Calfsound 49 E2
Calgary 36 B2
Callander 38 A4
Callington 4 B2
Calne 14 B4
Calver 20 C1
Calverton 21 E2
Calvine 38 B2
Cam 14 A3
Camasnacroise 37 D2
Camberley 9 F1
Camberwell 51 E4
Camborne 3 E3
Cambridge 16 B2
Cambridge Airport 16 B2

Camelford 4 A2
Camer 51 H5
Campbeltown 32 C3
Camptown 35 D4
Camrose 12 A1
Cannich 41 E3
Cannington 7 E3
Cannock 20 B3
Canonbie 29 F1
Canterbury 11 E2
Canton 7 E2
Canvey Island 11 D1
Canwell Hall 53 D1
Caolas 36 A2
Caolas Scalpaigh 47 E3
Capel 10 B3
Capel Curig 18 C2
Capel St. Mary 17 D2
Cappercleuch 34 B3
Capplegill 34 B4
Caputh 38 C3
Carbost (Loch Harport)
   High. 40 B3
Carbost (Loch Snizort Beag)
   High. 40 B3
Carcroft 26 B3
Cardenden 39 D4
Cardiff 7 E2
Cardiff International Airport
   7 D2
Cardigan 12 A3
Cardross 33 E1
Cargenbridge 29 D1
Cargill 38 C3
Carlabhagh 47 E1
Carlisle 29 F2
Carlops 34 B2
Carlton Leics. 53 F1
Carlton Notts. 21 E2
Carlton Colville 23 F4
Carlton in Lindrick 26 B3
Carlton-on-Trent 21 E1
Carluke 34 A2
Carmarthen 12 B4
Carmyllie 39 E3
Carnbee 39 E4
Carnbo 38 C4
Carnforth 24 C1
Carno 13 D1
Carnoustie 39 E3
Carnwath 34 A2
Carradale 32 C3
Carrbridge 42 B4
Carronbridge 34 A4
Carsaig 36 C3
Carshalton 50 D5
Carsluith 28 C2
Carspharn 33 F4
Carstairs 34 A2
Carterton 14 C3
Cartmel 24 C1
Castle Bromwich 20 C4
Castle Bromwich 53 D3
Castle Carrock 30 A2
Castle Cary 8 A2
Castle Donnington 21 D3
Castle Douglas 29 D2
Castle End 53 E4
Castle Kennedy 28 A2
Castlebay (Bagh a'
   Chaisteil) 46 A4
Castleford 26 A3
Castlemartin 12 A2
Castleside 30 C2
Castleton N.Yorks. 31 E4
Castletown High. 45 E1
Castletown I.o.M. 24 A3

Caterham 10 B2
Catford 51 E4
Caton 25 D1
Catrine 33 F3
Catshill 14 B1
Catshill 52 B4
Catterick 30 C4
Catterick Camp 30 C4
Caunsall 52 A3
Caverswall 20 B2
Cawdor 42 A2
Cawood 26 B2
Cawston 23 E3
Caythorpe 21 F2
Cayton 27 D1
Ceann a'Bháigh 46 A1
Cearsiadar 47 E2
Cefn-mawr 19 E2
Ceres 39 D4
Cerrigydrudion 19 D2
Chad Valley 52 C3
Chadderton 25 E4
Chaddesley Corbett 52 A4
Chadwell St. Mary 51 H4
Chadwick End 53 E4
Chagford 4 C1
Chailey 10 B3
Chalfont Common 50 B2
Chalfont St. Giles 10 A1
Chalfont St. Giles 50 A2
Chalfont St. Peter 50 B2
Chalford 14 B3
Chalgrove 15 E4
Chalk 51 H4
Champany 34 A1
Chandler's Cross 50 B2
Chapel End 53 F2
Chapel Fields 53 F4
Chapel St. Leonards 22 B1
Chapel-en-le-Frith 25 F4
Chapelhall 34 A2
Chapeltown S.Yorks.
   26 A4
Chard 5 F1
Chardstock 5 F1
Charfield 14 A4
Charing 11 E2
Charlbury 15 D3
Charlestown 43 F4
Charlestown of Aberlour
   42 C3
Charlesworth 25 E4
Charlton Gt.Lon. 51 F4
Charlton Hants. 9 D1
Charlton Wilts. 14 B4
Charlton Kings 14 B3
Charlwood 10 B3
Charminster 8 A3
Charmouth 5 F1
Chartham 11 E2
Chartridge 50 A1
Chasetown 52 C1
Chatham 11 D2
Chatteris 22 B4
Chatton 35 E3
Cheadle Gt.Man. 25 E4
Cheadle Staffs. 20 B2
Cheam 50 D5
Cheapside 50 A5
Checkley Staffs. 20 B2
Chedburgh 16 C2
Cheddar 7 F3
Cheddleton 20 B2
Chelmorton 20 C1
Chelmsford 16 C3
Chelsfield 51 F5
Cheltenham 14 B3

Chenies 50 B2
Chepstow 7 F1
Cheriton 9 E2
Chertsey 10 A2
Chertsey 50 B5
Chesham 15 F3
Chesham 50 A1
Chesham Bois 50 A2
Cheshunt 16 B4
Cheshunt 51 E1
Cheslyn Hay 52 B1
Chessington 50 C5
Chester 19 F2
Chester-le-Street 31 D2
Chesterfield Derbys.
   21 D1
Chesterfield Staffs. 53 D1
Chesters 35 D4
Chew Magna 8 A1
Chichester 9 F3
Chickerell 8 A4
Chiddingfold 9 F2
Chieveley 15 D4
Chignall St. James 51 H1
Chigwell 10 C1
Chigwell 51 F2
Chigwell Row 51 F2
Chilcompton 8 A1
Childerditch 51 H3
Childrey 15 D4
Chilham 11 E2
Chilton 31 D3
Chilvers Coton 53 F2
Chingford 10 B1
Chingford 51 E2
Chinnor 15 E3
Chippenham 14 B4
Chipperfield 50 B1
Chipping Campden 14 C2
Chipping Norton 14 C2
Chipping Ongar 16 B4
Chipping Ongar 51 G1
Chipping Sodbury 14 A4
Chirbury 13 E1
Chirk 19 E3
Chirnside 35 E2
Chiseldon 14 C4
Chislehurst 51 F4
Chiswell Green 50 C1
Chiswick 50 D4
Chobham 50 A5
Cholesbury 50 A1
Chopwell 30 C2
Chorley 25 D3
Chorleywood 15 F4
Chorleywood 50 B2
Christchurch Dorset 8 C4
Christon Bank 35 F3
Chryston 33 F1
Chudleigh 5 D2
Chulmleigh 6 C4
Church Aston 20 A3
Church End Warks. 53 E2
Church Lawton 20 B1
Church Stretton 13 F1
Churchdown 14 B3
Churchgate 51 E1
Churchill H. & W. 52 A4
Cilcain 19 E2
Cille Bhrighde 46 A3
Cinderford 14 A3
Cirencester 14 B3
City of London 51 E4
City of Westminster 50 D3
Clabhach 36 A2
Clachan (Kintyre) Arg. & B.
   32 C2

Clachan (Loch Fyne)
   Arg. & B. 37 E4
Clachan (Raasay) High.
   40 B3
Clachan of Glendaruel
   33 D1
Clachtoll 44 A3
Clackmannan 34 A1
Clacton-on-Sea 17 E3
Cladich 37 E3
Claggan 37 D2
Clanfield Oxon. 14 C3
Claonaig 32 C2
Clapham Beds. 15 F1
Clapham Gt.Lon. 50 D4
Clapham N.Yorks. 25 D1
Clarborough 26 B4
Clare 16 C2
Clashmore 42 A1
Clashnessie 44 A3
Clatterford End 51 G1
Claverdon 53 D5
Clavering 16 B3
Clay Cross 21 D1
Claydon 17 E2
Claygate Surr. 50 C5
Clayhanger W.Mid. 52 C1
Claypole 21 F2
Clayton W.Suss. 10 B4
Clayton West 25 F3
Clayton-le-Moors 25 D3
Clayton-le-Woods 25 D3
Cleadale 36 C1
Cleadon 31 D1
Cleat 49 E4
Cleator Moor 29 E3
Cleckheaton 25 F3
Cleehill 14 A1
Cleethorpes 27 E3
Clehonger 13 F4
Cleland 34 A2
Clenchwarton 22 B3
Clent 20 B4
Clent 52 B4
Cleobury Mortimer 14 A1
Clestrain 49 D3
Clevedon 7 F2
Cleveleys 24 C2
Clewer Village 50 A4
Cliffe 11 D1
Cliffe Woods 11 D1
Clipstone 21 E1
Clitheroe 25 D2
Closeburn 34 A4
Cloughton 31 F4
Clova 39 D1
Clovelly 6 B4
Clovenfords 34 C3
Clovullin 37 E2
Clowne 21 D1
Clun 13 E2
Clunes 37 E1
Clutton 8 A1
Clydach 6 C1
Clydebank 33 F1
Clynderwen 12 A4
Clyro 13 E3
Coalburn 34 A3
Coalville 21 D3
Coast 41 D1
Coatbridge 33 F2
Cobham Kent 51 H5
Cobham Surr. 10 A2
Cock Bridge 42 C4
Cockburnspath 35 D1
Cockenzie & Port Seton
   34 C1

Cockerham 24 C2
Cockermouth 29 E3
Cockett 6 C1
Cockfield 30 C3
Cockfosters 50 D2
Coddenham 17 E2
Coddington 21 F1
Codicote 16 A3
Codnor 21 D2
Codsall 20 B3
Codsall 52 A1
Codsall Wood 52 A1
Cofton Hackett 52 C4
Coggeshall 17 D3
Colchester 17 D3
Coldblow 51 G4
Colden Common 9 E2
Coldingham 35 E2
Coldstream 35 E3
Coleford 14 A3
Colehill 8 C3
Coleshill Bucks. 50 A2
Coleshill Warks. 20 C4
Coleshill Warks. 53 E3
Colintraive 33 D1
Collafirth 48 B2
Collier Row 51 G2
Collieston 43 F3
Collin 29 E1
Collingham 21 F1
Collycroft 53 F3
Colmonell 28 A1
Colnabaichin 42 C4
Colnbrook 10 A1
Colnbrook 50 B4
Colne 25 E2
Colney Heath 16 A4
Colney Heath 50 D1
Colney Street 50 C1
Colquhar 34 C2
Colsterworth 21 F3
Coltishall 23 E3
Colwich 20 B3
Colwick 21 E2
Colwyn Bay 18 C1
Colyford 5 E1
Colyton 5 E1
Combe Martin 6 C3
Combe St. Nicholas 7 E4
Comberford 53 D1
Comberton 16 B2
Comrie 38 B3
Congdon's Shop 4 B2
Congerstone 53 F1
Congleton 20 B1
Congresbury 7 F2
Coningsby 22 A2
Conisbrough 26 A4
Coniston 29 F4
Connah's Quay 19 E1
Connel 37 D3
Conon Bridge 41 F2
Consett 30 C2
Constantine 3 F2
Contin 41 F2
Conwy 18 C1
Cookham 15 F4
Cookley H. & W. 20 B4
Cookley H. & W. 52 A3
Cooksmill Green 51 H1
Coombe Bissett 8 C2
Cooper's Hill 50 A4
Coopersale Common 51 F1
Copley 30 C3
Copplestone 5 D1
Coppull 25 D3
Copt Heath 53 D4

opythorne 9 D3
orbridge 30 B1
orby 21 F4
orfe Castle 8 C4
orfe Mullen 8 C3
orley 53 E3
orley Ash 53 E3
orley Moor 53 E3
ornhill 43 D2
ornhill-on-Tweed 35 E3
ornholme 25 E3
orpach 37 E1
orrie 33 D3
orringham 11 D1
orsham 8 B1
orsock 29 D1
orton 23 F4
orwen 19 D2
oryton 11 D1
osby 21 D4
oseley 52 B2
oshieville 38 B2
otgrave 21 E2
oton *Staffs.* **53 D1**
ottenham 16 B1
otteridge 52 C3
ottesmore 21 F3
ottingham *E.Riding*
  27 D2
ottingham *Northants.*
  21 F4
oulport 33 E1
oundon 30 C3
oupar Angus 39 D3
ourt House Green 53 F3
ove *Arg. & B.* 33 E1
ove *High.* 40 C1
ove Bay 43 F4
oven 52 B1
oventry 21 D4
oventry 53 F4
oventry Airport 53 F4
overack 3 F4
owbit 22 A3
owbridge 7 D2
owdenbeath 34 B1
owes 9 E3
owfold 10 B3
owie 34 A1
owley Gt.Lon. 50 B3
owling 25 E2
owshill 30 B2
oxheath 11 D2
oxtie Green 51 G2
oxwold 26 B1
oychurch 7 D2
oylton 33 E3
oylumbridge 42 B4
rabbs Cross 52 C5
radley *H. & W.* 14 A2
radley W.Mid. 52 B3
aichie 39 E2
aig 41 D3
aigandaive 33 D1
aigdarroch 33 F4
aigellachie 42 C3
aigendoran 33 E1
aighat 33 F1
aignure 37 D3
ail 39 E4
amlington 31 D1
amond 34 B1
anage 20 A1
anbourne 50 A4
anfield 15 F2
anford Gt.Lon. 50 C4
anham *Gt.Lon.* **51 G3**

Cranleigh 10 A3
Cranshaws 35 D2
Cranwell 21 F2
Crask Inn 44 C3
Craster 35 F3
Crathie 39 D1
Craven Arms 13 F2
Crawfordjohn 34 A3
Crawley 10 B3
Crayford 51 G4
Creag Ghoraidh 46 B2
Credenhill 13 F3
Crediton 5 D1
Creekmouth 51 F3
Creetown 28 C2
Cregneish 24 A3
Creswell 21 D1
Crewe 20 A1
Crewkerne 5 F1
Crianlarich 37 F3
Criccieth 18 B3
Crickhowell 13 E4
Cricklade 14 C4
Crieff 38 B3
Crigglestone 26 A3
Crimond 43 F2
Crinan 37 D4
Cringleford 23 E4
Cripp's Corner 11 D3
Crockenhill 51 G5
Crocketford or Ninemile
  Bar 29 D1
Croeserw 7 D1
Crofton 26 A3
Crofty 6 B1
Cromarty 42 A2
Cromer 23 E2
Cromford 20 C1
Cromhall 14 A4
Crondall 9 F1
Crook 30 C3
Crookham 35 E3
Crosbost 47 E2
Crosby *Mersey.* 24 C4
Crosby *N.Lincs.* 26 C3
Crosby Ravensworth
  30 A3
Cross Inn 12 C3
Crossaig 32 C2
Crosscanonby 29 E2
Crossford Fife 34 B1
Crossford *S.Lan.* 34 A2
Crossgates *Fife* 34 B1
Crossgates *Powys* 13 E3
Crosshands 33 F3
Crosshill 33 E4
Crosshouse 33 E3
Crossmichael 28 C1
Crossway 13 D3
Crossway Green 52 A5
Croston 26 A2
Croughton 15 D2
Crow Hill 14 A2
Crowborough 10 C3
Crowland 22 A3
Crowle 26 C3
Crowthorne 9 F1
Croxley Green 50 B2
Croy *High.* 42 A3
Croy *N.Lan.* 33 F1
Croyde 6 B3
Croydon Gt.Lon. 51 E5
Cruden Bay 43 F2
Crulabhig 47 E2
Crumlin 7 E1
Crymych 12 A4
Crynant 6 C1

Crystal Palace 51 E4
Cubbington 15 D1
Cubbington 53 F5
Cuckfield 10 B3
Cuddington *Ches.* 19 F1
Cudworth 26 A3
Cuffley 16 A4
Cuffley 51 E1
Culbokie 41 F2
Culcheth 19 F1
Culdrain 43 D3
Cullen 43 D2
Cullicudden 42 A2
Cullingworth 25 F2
Cullipool 37 D4
Cullivoe 48 C1
Cullompton 5 E1
Culmstock 7 E4
Culnacraig 44 A4
Culnaknock 40 B2
Culross 34 A1
Culswick 48 B3
Cults 43 E4
Culverstone Green 51 H5
Cumbernauld 34 A1
Cuminestown 43 E2
Cumnock 33 F3
Cumnor 15 D3
Cunningsburgh 48 B4
Cupar 39 D4
Curdworth 53 D2
Curry Rivel 7 F4
Cutnall Green 52 A5
Cwm 7 E1
Cwmafan 6 C1
Cwmbran 7 E1
Cwmllynfell 6 C1
Cydweli (Kidwelly) 6 B1
Cymmer 7 D1
Cynghordy 13 D4
Cynwyl Elfed 12 B4

D

Dacre 29 F3
Dagenham 51 F3
Dail Bho Thuath 47 F1
Dailly 33 E4
Dairsie 39 D4
Dalabrog 46 A3
Dalbeattie 29 D2
Dalby 24 A3
Dale *Pembs.* 12 A2
Dalgety Bay 34 B1
Dalham 16 C1
Dalkeith 34 C2
Dallas 42 B2
Dalmally 37 E3
Darenth 51 G4
Darfield 26 A4
Darlaston 52 B2
Darlington 31 D3
Darra 43 E3
Dartford 10 C1
Dartford 51 G4

Dartington 5 D2
Dartmeet 4 C2
Dartmouth 5 D3
Darton 26 A3
Darvel 33 F3
Darwen 25 D3
Datchet 50 A4
Dava 42 B3
Davenham 20 A1
Daventry 15 D1
Daviot 42 A3
Dawlish 5 D2
Deal 11 F2
Dearham 29 E3
Debenham 17 E1
Dechmont 34 A1
Deddington 15 D2
Dedham 17 D2
Deeping St. James 22 A3
Deeping St. Nicholas
  22 A3
Deganwy 18 C1
Delabole 4 A1
Delamere 19 F2
Denbigh 19 D2
Denby Dale 25 F3
Denham *Bucks.* 10 A1
Denham Bucks. 50 B3
Denham Green 50 B3
Denholm 35 D3
Denholme 25 F2
Denmead 9 E3
Dennington 17 E1
Denny 34 A1
Denton 25 E4
Denver 22 C4
Deptford Gt.Lon. 51 E4
Derby 21 D2
Dersingham 22 C3
Dervaig 36 C2
Desborough 21 E4
Devil's Bridge 12 C2
Devizes 8 C2
Dewsbury 25 F3
Dhoon 24 B2
Dibden 9 D3
Didcot 15 D4
Dinas Powys 7 E2
Dingwall 41 F2
Dinnet 43 D4
Dinnington *S.Yorks.* 26 B4
Dippen 32 C3
Dirleton 34 C1
Diss 17 E1
Distington 29 E3
Ditton *Kent* 11 D2
Dobwalls 4 A2
Dochgarroch 41 F3
Docking 22 C2
Doddinghurst 51 G2
Doddington 35 E3
Dodford H. & W. 52 B4
Dodington 14 A4
Dodworth 26 A4
Dogdyke 22 A2
Dolanog 13 E1
Dolbenmaen 18 B3
Dolfor 13 E2
Dolgarrog 18 C2
Dolgellau 12 C1
Dollar 38 B4
Dolphinton 34 B2
Doncaster 26 B4
Donington 22 A2
Donkey Town 50 A5
Donnington *Shrop.* 20 A3
Dorchester 8 A4

Dordon 20 C4
Dordon 53 E1
Dores 41 F3
Dorking 10 B2
Dorney 50 A4
Dornie 41 D3
Dornoch 42 A1
Dorridge 53 D4
Dosthill 53 E1
Dougarie 32 C3
Douglas *I.o.M.* 24 B3
Douglas *S.Lan.* 34 A3
Douglastown 39 D2
Dounby 49 D3
Doune 38 B4
Dounreay 45 E1
Dover 11 F3
Doverdale 52 A5
Doveridge 20 C2
Dowally 38 C2
Downe 51 F5
Downham Market 22 C4
Downton 8 C2
Dowsby 22 A3
Drakes Cross 52 C4
Drayton H. & W. 52 B4
Drayton *Norf.* 23 E3
Drayton *Oxon.* 15 D4
Drayton Bassett 53 D1
Drefach 6 B1
Dreghorn 33 E3
Drem 34 C1
Drimnin 36 C2
Droitwich 14 B1
Droitwich 52 A5
Dronfield 21 D1
Drongan 33 F3
Dropmore 50 A3
Droylsden 25 E4
Druid 19 D3
Druimdrishaig 32 C1
Drumbeg 44 A2
Drumclog 33 F3
Drumlithie 39 F1
Drummore 28 A2
Drumnadrochit 41 F3
Drybrook 14 A3
Drymen 33 F1
Duddo 35 E2
Dudley *W.Mid.* 20 B4
Dudley W.Mid. 52 B2
Dudley Port 52 B2
Duffield 21 D2
Dufftown 42 C3
Duirinish 40 C3
Dullingham 16 C2
Dulnain Bridge 42 B3
Dulverton 7 D4
Dulwich 51 E4
Dumbarton 33 E1
Dumfries 29 D1
Dunbar 35 D1
Dunbeath 45 E3
Dunblane 38 B4
Dunchurch 15 D1
Dundee 39 D3
Dundonald 33 E3
Dundreggan 41 E4
Dundrennan 29 D2
Dunecht 43 E4
Dunfermline 34 B1
Dunhampton 52 A5
Dunholme 21 F1
Dunkeld 38 C3
Dunkirk 11 E2
Dunlop 33 E2
Dunnet 45 E1

Dunning 38 C4
Dunoon 33 D1
Dunragit 28 A2
Duns 35 D2
Dunscore 29 D1
Dunstable 15 F3
Dunster 7 D3
Dunton Wayletts 51 H3
Dunure 33 E4
Dunvant 6 C1
Dunvegan 40 A3
Durham 31 D2
Durness 44 B1
Durrington 8 C1
Dursley 14 A3
Dyce 43 E4
Dyke 42 B2
Dykehead 39 D2
Dymchurch 11 E3
Dymock 14 A2
Dyserth 19 D1

E

Eaglescliffe 31 D3
Eaglesfield 29 E1
Eaglesham 33 F2
Ealing 50 C3
Earby 25 E2
Eardisley 13 E3
Earith 16 B1
Earl Shilton 21 D4
Earl Stonham 17 E2
Earls Barton 15 F1
Earls Colne 17 D3
Earlsdon 53 F4
Earlston 35 D3
Earlswood Warks. 53 D4
Earsairidh 46 A4
Easdale 37 D4
Easebourne 9 F2
Easington Dur. 31 D2
Easington E.Riding 27 F3
Easington Colliery 31 D2
Easingwold 26 B1
East Barnet 50 D2
East Bedfont 50 B4
East Bergholt 17 D2
East Bridgford 21 E2
East Calder 34 B1
East Dereham 23 D3
East Goscote 21 E3
East Grinstead 10 B3
East Ham 51 F3
East Hanney 15 D4
East Harling 23 D4
East Haven 39 E3
East Horndon 51 H3
East Horsley 10 A2
East Huntspill 7 F3
East Keal 22 B1
East Kilbride 33 F2
East Leake 21 D3
East Linton 35 D1
East Malling 11 D2
East Markham 21 E1
East Midlands International
   Airport 21 D2
East Molesey 50 C5
East Preston 10 A4
East Retford (Retford)
   21 E1
East Wemyss 39 D4
East Wickham 51 F4
East Wittering 9 F3
Eastbury Herts. 50 C2

Eastcote Gt.Lon. 50 C3
Eastcote W.Mid. 53 D4
Easter Lednathie 39 D2
Easter Quarff 48 B4
Eastfield 27 D1
Eastgate 30 B2
Eastleigh Hants. 9 D3
Eastoft 26 C3
Easton 8 A4
Easton on the Hill 21 F3
Easton-in-Gordano 7 F2
Eastriggs 29 F1
Eastry 11 F2
Eastwood Notts. 21 D2
Eathorpe 53 F5
Eaton Socon 16 A1
Ebbw Vale 7 E1
Ecclaw 35 D1
Ecclefechan 29 E1
Eccles Sc.Bord. 35 D2
Ecclesfield 26 A4
Eccleshall 20 B2
Eccleston Lancs. 25 D3
Echt 43 E4
Eckford 35 D3
Eckington Derbys. 21 D1
Eckington H. & W. 14 B2
Edderton 42 A1
Eddleston 34 B2
Eden Park 51 E5
Edenbridge 10 C2
Edenfield 25 E3
Edgbaston 52 C3
Edgware 50 D2
Edgworth 25 D3
Edial 52 C1
Edinburgh 34 B1
Edinburgh Airport 34 B1
Edlingham 35 F4
Edmonton 51 E2
Edmundbyers 30 C2
Edney Common 51 H1
Edstone 53 D5
Edwinstowe 21 E1
Edzell 39 E2
Egglescliffe 31 D3
Egham 10 A1
Egham 50 B4
Eglingham 35 F3
Eglwys Fach 12 C1
Eglwyswrw 12 A4
Egremont 29 E3
Egton 31 F4
Einacleit 47 D2
Elgin 42 C2
Elgol 40 B4
Elham 11 E2
Elie 39 E4
Eling 9 D3
Elland 25 F3
Ellesmere 19 E3
Ellesmere Port 19 F1
Ellingham 35 F3
Ellington 35 F4
Ellon 43 F3
Elloughton 26 C3
Elm Park 51 G3
Elmbridge 52 B5
Elmdon W.Mid. 53 D3
Elmdon Heath 53 D3
Elmley Lovett 52 A5
Elmswell 17 D1
Elmton 21 D1
Elphin 44 B3
Elsdon 35 E4
Elsrickle 34 B2

Elstead 9 F2
Elstree 16 A4
Elstree 50 C2
Elswick 24 C2
Eltham 51 F4
Elton Cambs. 22 A4
Elton Ches. 19 F1
Elvanfoot 34 A3
Elvington 26 B2
Ely Cambs. 16 B1
Ely Cardiff 7 E2
Embleton 35 F3
Emsworth 9 F3
Enderby 21 D4
Endon 20 B2
Enfield 51 E2
Englefield Green 50 A4
Enstone 15 D2
Enterkinfoot 34 A4
Enville 52 A3
Eoropaidh 47 F1
Epping 16 B4
Epping 51 F1
**Epping Green Essex
   51 F1**
**Epping Green Herts.
   50 D1**
Epping Upland 51 F1
Epsom 10 B2
Epsom 50 D5
Epworth 26 C4
Erdington 53 D2
Eriboll 44 B2
Eriswell 16 C1
Erith 51 G4
Errogie 41 F4
Errol 39 D3
Esh Winning 30 C2
Esher 10 A2
Esher 50 B1
Eskdalemuir 34 B4
Essendon 50 D1
Essington 52 B1
Eston 31 E3
Eton 10 A1
Eton 50 A4
Eton Wick 50 A4
Etteridge 38 A1
Ettington 14 C2
Ettingshall 52 B2
Ettrick 34 B4
Ettrickbridge 34 C3
Euxton 25 D3
Evanton 41 F2
Evercreech 8 A2
Evesham 14 B2
Ewell 10 B2
Ewell 50 D5
Ewhurst 10 A3
Exebridge 7 D4
Exeter 5 D1
Exminster 5 D1
Exmouth 5 E2
Eye Cambs. 22 A4
Eye Suff. 17 E1
Eyemouth 35 E2
Eynsford 10 C2
Eynsford 51 G5
Eynsham 15 D3

F

Failsworth 25 E4
Fair Oak Hants. 9 E3
Fairfield H. & W. 52 B4
Fairford 14 C3
Fairlie 33 E2

Fairlight 11 D4
Fairseat 51 H5
Fakenham 23 D3
Falkirk 34 A1
Falkland 39 D4
Fallin 34 A1
Falmouth 3 F3
Falstone 30 A1
Fareham 9 E3
Faringdon 14 C4
Farington 25 D3
Farleigh Surr. 51 E5
Farmborough 8 A1
**Farnborough Gt.Lon.
   51 F5**
Farnborough Hants. 9 F1
Farndon 21 E2
Farnham 9 F1
Farnham Common 50 A3
Farnham Royal 10 A1
Farnham Royal 50 A3
Farningham 51 G5
Farnsfield 21 E1
Farnworth Gt.Man. 25 D3
Farr 42 A3
Fauldhouse 34 A2
Faversham 11 E2
Fawkham Green 51 G5
Fawley Hants. 9 D3
Fazeley 20 C4
Fazeley 53 E1
Fearnhead 19 F1
Fearnmore 40 C2
Featherstone Staffs.
   20 B3
**Featherstone Staffs.
   52 B1**
Featherstone W.Yorks.
   26 A3
Felden 50 B1
Felindre 13 E2
Felixstowe 17 E2
Felling 31 D1
Felsted 16 C3
Feltham 50 C4
Felton 35 F4
Feltwell 22 C4
Fen End 53 E4
Feniton 5 E1
Fenny Drayton 53 F2
Fenstanton 16 A1
Fenwick E.Ayr. 33 F2
Fenwick Nhumb. 35 F2
Feochaig 32 C4
Feolin Ferry 32 B2
Fern 39 E2
Ferndown 8 C3
Ferness 42 B3
Fernhill Heath 14 B1
Fernhurst 9 F2
Ferryden 39 E2
Ferryhill 31 D3
Feshiebridge 42 A4
Fettercairn 39 E1
Ffestiniog 18 C3
Ffostrasol 12 B3
Fiddlers Hamlet 51 F1
Filey 27 F3
Fillongley 20 C4
Fillongley 53 E3
Filton 14 A4
Fimber 26 C1
Finavon 39 E2
Finchampstead 9 F1
Finchingfield 16 C3
Finchley 50 D2
Findern 20 C2

Findhorn 42 B2
Findochty 43 D2
Findon 10 A4
Finedon 15 F1
Finningham 17 D1
Finningley 26 B4
Finnygaud 43 D2
Finsbury 51 E3
Finstall 52 B4
Finstown 49 E3
Fintry 33 F1
Fionnphort 36 B3
Fishburn 31 D3
Fishguard 12 B1
Fishnish 36 C3
Fiunary 36 C2
Flackwell Heath 15 F4
Flamborough 27 D1
Flamstead End 51 E1
Flaunden 50 B1
Fleet 9 F1
Fleetwood 24 C2
Flempton 16 C1
Flimby 29 E3
Flimwell 11 D3
Flint 19 E1
Flitwick 15 F2
Flodden 35 E3
Flookburgh 24 C1
Fochabers 42 C2
Foleshill 53 F3
Folkestone 11 F3
Folkingham 21 F2
Folly Gate 4 C1
Foots Cray 51 F4
Ford Arg. & B. 37 D4
Ford Nhumb. 35 E3
Fordham 16 C1
Fordingbridge 8 C3
Fordoun 39 F1
Fordyce 43 D2
Forest Gate 51 F3
Forest Row 10 C3
Forfar 39 D2
Forgandenny 38 C3
Forgie 42 C2
Formby 24 C3
Forres 42 B2
Forsbrook 20 B2
Forsinard 45 D2
Fort Augustus 41 E4
Fort William 37 E1
Forth 34 A2
Fortingall 38 B2
Fortrose 42 A2
Fortuneswell 8 A4
Forty Green 50 A2
Forty Hill 51 E2
Foster Street 51 F1
Fotherby 27 E4
Foulden 35 E2
Foulridge 25 E2
Four Ashes Staffs. 52 B1
**Four Crosses Staffs.
   52 B1**
Four Elms 10 C2
Four Marks 9 E2
Four Oaks E.Suss. 11 D3
**Four Oaks (Meriden)
   W.Mid. 53 E3**
**Four Oaks (Sutton Coldfield)
   W.Mid. 53 D2**
Fowey 4 A3
Fownhope 14 A2
Foxdale 24 A3
Foyers 41 F4
Framfield 10 C3

mlingham 17 E1
mpton Cotterell 14 A4
mpton on Severn 14 A3
anche 52 A4
ankley 20 B4
ankley 52 B3
aserburgh 43 F2
ckleton 24 C3
emington 6 B4
eshwater 9 D4
eshwater East 12 B2
ssingfield 17 E1
swick 45 F1
euchie 39 D4
daythorpe 26 C1
ern Barnet 50 D2
nley 9 F1
nton-on-Sea 17 E3
ockheim 39 E2
helstock Stone 6 B4
zington 29 E3
dsham 19 F1
gmore Hants. 9 F1
gmore Herts. 50 C1
me 8 B1
erning 51 H1
bourn 16 B2
ford Staffs. 20 B2
ford York 26 B2
ham 10 B1
lham 50 D4
mer 50 A3
wood Lancs. 25 D2
nzie 48 C1
rnace 37 E4
ield Essex 16 B3
ield Essex 51 G1
vie 43 E3

er 13 E4
nford 30 C3
insborough 26 C4
irloch 40 C1
ashiels 34 C3
ley Common 53 F2
llowstree Elm 52 A3
misdale 36 C1
lston 33 F3
nlingay 16 A2
denstown 43 E2
rderhouse 48 B3
relochhead 33 E1
rforth 26 A2
grave 25 E2
rlieston 28 C2
rsdale Head 30 B4
rstang 24 C2
rth 13 D3
rthmyl 13 E1
rtocharn 33 E1
rvald 35 D1
rvamore 38 A1
rvard 32 A1
rve 41 F2
tehouse of Fleet 28 C2
teshead 31 D2
tley 25 E4
twick (London) Airport
10 B3
wthrop 30 A4
yton 22 C3
arraidh na h-Aibhne
47 E2
ddington 21 F4
dney 22 B3

Gelligaer 7 E1
George Green 50 B3
Georgeham 6 B3
Gerrards Cross 10 A1
Gerrards Cross 50 A3
Gidea Park 51 G3
Giffnock 33 F2
Gifford 34 C1
Gilberdyke 26 C3
Gillamoor 31 E4
Gilling West 30 C4
Gillingham Dorset 8 B2
Gillingham Kent 11 D2
Gilmerton 38 B3
Gilsland 30 A1
Gilston 34 C2
Gilwern 7 E1
Girlsta 48 B3
Girvan 33 E4
Gisburn 25 E2
Glamis 39 D2
Glanaman 6 C1
Glanton 35 E3
Glasbury 13 E4
Glascote 53 E1
Glasgow 33 F2
Glasgow Airport 33 F2
Glassford 33 F2
Glastonbury 7 F3
Glemsford 16 C2
Glen Vine 24 A3
Glenbarr 32 B3
Glenbeg 36 C2
Glenborrodale 36 C2
Glenbreck 34 B3
Glenbrittle 40 B4
Glencaple 29 E1
Glencarse 38 C3
Glencoe 37 E2
Gleneagles 38 B4
Glenegedale 32 A2
Glenelg 40 C4
Glenfarg 38 C4
Glenfield 21 D3
Glenfinnan 37 D1
Glengarnock 33 E2
Glenkindie 43 D4
Glenluce 28 A2
Glenrothes 39 D4
Glinton 22 A4
Glossop 25 F4
Gloucester 14 B3
Glusburn 25 E2
Glyn Ceiriog 19 E3
Glyn-Neath 7 D1
Glyncorrwg 7 D1
Gnosall 20 B3
Gobowen 19 E3
Godalming 10 A2
Godmanchester 16 A1
Godstone 10 B2
Goff's Oak 51 E1
Golborne 25 D4
Goldcliff 7 F2
Golden Pot 9 F2
Golders Green 50 D3
Golspie 45 D4
Goodwick 12 A1
Goodyers End 53 F3
Goole 26 B3
Goonhavern 3 F2
Gorcott Hill 52 C5
Gordon 35 D2
Gorebridge 34 C2
Goring 15 E4
Gornalwood 52 B2
Gorseinon 6 C1

Gosberton 22 A3
Gosfield 16 C3
Gosforth Cumb. 29 E4
Gosforth T. & W. 30 C1
Gospel End 52 B2
Gosport 9 E3
Gotham 21 D2
Goudhurst 11 D3
Gourdon 39 F2
Goxhill 27 D3
Grabhair 47 E2
Grain 11 D1
Grampound 3 F3
Grandtully 38 B2
Grange Hill 51 F2
Grange-over-Sands 24 C1
Grangemouth 34 A1
Grantham 21 F2
Grantown-on-Spey 42 B3
Grantshouse 35 D2
Grasmere 29 F4
Grassington 25 E1
Gravelly Hill 53 D2
Gravesend 10 C1
Gravesend 51 H4
Grayrigg 30 A4
Grays 10 C1
Grays 51 H4
Grayshott 9 F2
Greasby 19 E1
Great Ayton 31 E3
Great Baddow 16 C3
Great Barr 52 C2
Great Barton 17 D1
Great Bircham 22 C3
Great Broughton 31 E4
Great Clifton 29 E3
Great Cornard 17 D2
Great Driffield 27 D2
Great Dunmow 16 C3
Great Eccleston 24 C2
Great Ellingham 23 D4
Great Glen 21 E4
Great Gonerby 21 F2
Great Gransden 16 A2
Great Hanwood 13 F1
Great Harwood 25 D2
Great Heath 53 F3
Great Horkesley 17 D3
Great Linford 15 F2
Great Malvern 14 A2
Great Marton 24 B2
Great Missenden 15 F3
Great Oxney Green 51 H1
Great Parndon 51 F1
Great Ponton 21 F2
Great Salkeld 30 A2
Great Sampford 16 C2
Great Sankey 19 F1
Great Shelford 16 B2
Great Torrington 6 B4
Great Wakering 11 E1
Great Warley 51 G2
Great Wyrley 20 B3
Great Wyrley 52 B1
Great Yarmouth 23 F4
Great Yeldham 16 C2
Greatham Hants. 9 F2
Greatstone-on-Sea 11 E3
Green Street 50 C2
Green Street Green Gt.Lon.
51 F5
Green Street Green Kent
51 G4
Greenford 50 C3
Greengairs 34 A1
Greenham 9 E1

Greenhead 30 A1
Greenhill Gt.Lon. 50 C3
Greenhithe 51 G4
Greenigo 49 E3
Greenlaw 35 D2
Greenloaning 38 B4
Greenock 33 E1
Greenodd 24 C1
Greensted 51 G1
Greenway 12 A4
Greenwich 51 E4
Grendon Warks. 53 E2
Grendon Common 53 E2
Gresford 19 E2
Gretna 29 F1
Greystoke 29 F3
Griais 47 F1
Griff 53 F3
Grimoldby 22 B1
Grimsby 27 D3
Grimston 22 C3
Gringley on the Hill 26 B4
Gritley 49 E3
Grizebeck 29 E4
Grove 15 D4
Grove Park 51 F4
Grudie 41 E2
Grutness 48 A4
Guide Post 30 C1
Guildford 10 A2
Guildtown 38 C3
Guisborough 31 E3
Guiseley 25 F2
Guist 23 D3
Gullane 34 C1
Gunness 26 C3
Gunnislake 4 B2
Gurnos 6 C1
Gutcher 48 C1
Gwaun-Cae-Gurwen 6 C1
Gwithian 3 E3
Gwytherin 18 C2

H

Hackleton 15 E1
Hacklinge 11 E2
Hackness 31 F4
Hackney 51 E3
Haddenham 16 B1
Haddington 34 C1
Haddiscoe 23 F4
Hademore 53 D1
Hadleigh 17 D2
Hadley 20 A3
Hadley Wood 50 D2
Hadzor 52 B5
Hagley (Hereford) H. & W.
14 A2
Hagley (Stourbridge)
H. & W. 20 B4
Hagley (Stourbridge)
H. & W. 52 B3
Hailsham 10 C4
Hainault 51 F2
Hale Gt.Man. 25 E4
Hales 23 F4
Halesowen 20 B4
Halesowen 52 B3
Halesworth 17 F1
Halewood 19 F1
Halfpenny Green 52 A2
Halifax 25 F3
Halkirk 45 E2
Halkyn 19 E1
Hall 33 E2
Hall Green 53 D3

Halland 10 C4
Hallow 14 B1
Hallworthy 4 A1
Halstead Essex 16 C3
Halstead Kent 51 F5
Halton Gill 25 E1
Haltwhistle 30 A1
Halwell 5 D3
Ham Gt.Lon. 50 C4
Ham Shet. 48 A3
Ham Green H. & W. 52 C5
Hamble-le-Rice 9 E3
Hambleton 24 C2
Hamilton 33 F2
Hammersmith & Fulham
50 C4
Hammerwich 52 C1
Hammond Street 51 E1
Hamnavoe (Mainland)
Shet. 48 B4
Hamnavoe (Yell) Shet.
48 C2
Hampreston 8 C3
Hampstead 50 D3
Hampton Gt.Lon. 50 C5
Hampton in Arden 53 E3
Hampton Lovett 52 A5
Hampton on the Hill 53 E5
Hamstead W.Mid. 52 C2
Hanbury H. & W. 52 B5
Handsacre 20 C3
Handsworth W.Mid.
52 C2
Hanham 14 A4
Hanley Castle 14 B2
Hanwell Gt.Lon. 50 C4
Hanworth Gt.Lon. 50 C4
Happisburgh 23 F3
Harbledown 11 E2
Harborne 52 C3
Harbury 15 D1
Hardingstone 15 E1
Hardwicke 14 A3
Hare Street 16 B3
Harefield 10 A1
Harefield 50 B2
Harewood 26 A2
Haringey 51 E3
Harlech 18 B3
Harlesden 50 D3
Harleston 23 E4
Harlington 15 F2
Harlow 16 B3
Harmondsworth 50 B4
Harmston 21 F1
Harold Hill 51 G2
Harold Wood 51 G2
Haroldswick 48 C1
Harpenden 16 A3
Harpole 15 E1
Harrietfield 38 C3
Harrietsham 11 D2
Harrogate 26 A2
Harrow Gt.Lon. 50 C3
Harrow on the Hill 50 C3
Harrow Weald 50 C2
Harston 16 B2
Hartfield 10 C3
Harthill N.Lan. 34 A2
Hartland 6 A4
Hartlebury 14 B1
Hartlebury 52 A4
Hartlepool 31 E3
Hartley Kent 10 C2
Hartley Kent 51 H5
Hartley Wintney 9 F1

Hartpury 14 A2
Hartshill 21 D4
Hartshill 53 F2
Hartshorne 21 D3
Harvel 51 H5
Harvington *H. & W.* 14 B2
Harvington *H. & W.* **52 A4**
Harwell 15 D4
Harwich 17 E3
Harworth 26 B4
Hasbury 52 B3
Haseley 53 E5
Hasland 21 D1
Haslemere 9 F2
Haslingden 25 E3
Hassendean 34 C3
Hastings 11 D4
Hastingwood 51 F1
Hastoe 50 A1
Haswell 31 D2
Hatch End 50 C2
Hatfield *Herts.* 16 A3
Hatfield *Herts.* 50 D1
Hatfield *S.Yorks.* 26 B3
Hatfield Broad Oak 16 B3
Hatfield Peverel 16 C3
Hatherleigh 4 C1
Hathern 21 D3
Hathersage 25 F4
Hatton *Aber.* 43 F3
Hatton *Derbys.* 20 C2
Hatton *Gt.Lon.* 50 B4
Hatton *Warks.* 53 E5
Haugh of Urr 29 D1
Haughton 20 B3
Havant 9 F3
Haverfordwest 12 A2
Haverhill 16 C2
Havering 51 G3
Havering-atte-Bower
51 G2
Hawarden 19 E2
Hawes 30 B4
Hawick 34 C3
Hawkes End 53 F3
Hawkhurst 11 D3
Hawkinge 11 F3
Hawkshead 29 F4
Hawkwell 11 D1
Hawley *Hants.* 9 F1
Hawley *Kent* 51 G4
Haworth 25 F2
Haxby 26 B1
Haxey 26 C4
Hay Mills 53 D3
Hay-on-Wye 13 E3
Haydock 25 D4
Haydon Bridge 30 B1
Haydon Wick 14 C4
Hayes (Bromley) *Gt.Lon.*
51 F5
Hayes (Hillingdon) *Gt.Lon.*
50 B3
Hayfield 25 F4
Hayle 3 E3
Hayton 26 C2
Haywards Heath 10 B3
Hazel Grove 25 E4
Hazelwood *Gt.Lon.* 51 F5
Hazlemere 15 F4
Heacham 22 C2
Headcorn 11 D2
Headless Cross 52 C5
Headley 9 F2
Healeyfield 30 C2
Healing 27 D3
Heanor 21 D2

Heath 21 D1
Heath Town 52 B2
Heathfield 10 C3
Heathrow (London) Airport
10 A1
Heathrow (London) Airport
50 B4
Heathton 52 A2
Hebburn 31 D1
Hebden Bridge 25 E3
Heckington 22 A2
Hedge End 9 E3
Hedgerley 50 A3
Hedon 27 D3
Heglibister 48 B3
Heighington 21 F1
Helensburgh 33 E1
Helhoughton 23 D3
Hellifield 25 E2
Helmsdale 45 E3
Helmsley 31 E4
Helpringham 22 A2
Helsby 19 F1
Helston 3 E3
Hemel Hempstead 16 A3
Hemel Hempstead 50 B1
Hemingford Grey 16 A1
Hempnall 23 E4
Hempstead 16 C2
Hemsby 23 F3
Hemsworth 26 A3
Hemyock 7 E4
Hendon *Gt.Lon.* 10 B1
Hendon *Gt.Lon.* 50 D3
Henfield 10 B4
Hengoed 7 E1
Henley-in-Arden 14 C1
Henley-in-Arden 53 D5
Henley-on-Thames
15 E4
Henlow 16 A2
Henstridge 8 B2
Hereford 13 F4
Heriot 34 C2
Herne Bay 11 E2
Herongate 51 H2
Heronsgate 50 B2
Hersham *Surr.* 50 C5
Herstmonceux 10 C4
Herston 49 E4
Hertford 16 B3
Heston 50 C4
Heswall 19 E1
Hethersett 23 E4
Hetton 25 E1
Hetton-le-Hole 31 D2
Hewell Grange 52 C5
Hewell Lane 52 C5
Hexham 30 B1
Hextable 10 C1
Hextable 51 G4
Heybridge (Ingatestone)
Essex 51 H2
Heybridge (Maldon) *Essex*
17 D3
Heysham 24 C1
Heywood 25 E3
Hibaldstow 26 C4
High Beach 51 F2
High Bentham 25 D1
High Blantyre 33 F2
High Bradfield 26 A4
High Etherley 30 C3
High Garrett 16 C3
High Halden 11 D3
High Hawsker 31 F4
High Hesket 29 F2

High Laver 51 G1
High Legh 25 D4
High Lorton 29 E3
High Ongar 51 G1
High Wycombe 15 F4
Higham 11 D1
Higham Ferrers 15 F1
Higham on the Hill 53 F2
Highampton 4 B1
Highbridge 7 E3
Highclere 9 D1
Higher Walton *Lancs.*
25 D3
Highley 20 A4
Highnam 14 A3
Highworth 14 C4
Hildenborough 10 C2
Hilgay 22 C4
Hill End 38 C4
Hill of Fearn 42 A1
Hillingdon 50 B3
Hillside *Angus* 39 E2
Hillside *Shet.* 48 B2
Hillswick 48 B2
Hilperton 8 B1
Hilton *Derbys.* 20 C2
Himley 52 A2
Hinckley 21 D4
Hinderwell 31 F3
Hindhead 9 F2
Hindley 25 D4
Hindon 8 B2
Hingham 23 D4
Hints *Staffs.* 53 D1
Hirwaun 7 D1
Histon 16 B1
Hitchin 16 A3
Hither Green 51 E4
Hockley 11 D1
Hockley Heath 14 C1
Hockley Heath 53 D4
Hoddesdon 16 B3
Hoddesdon 51 E1
Hodnet 19 F3
Hogsthorpe 22 B1
Holbeach 22 B3
Holbrook *Suff.* 17 E2
Holden 25 E2
Holland-on-Sea 17 E3
Hollington 11 D4
Hollingworth 25 F4
Hollybush *E.Ayr.* 33 E4
Hollybush *H. & W.* 14 A2
Holme-on-Spalding-Moor
26 C2
Holmes Chapel 20 A1
Holmesfield 20 C1
Holmfirth 25 F3
Holsworthy 4 B1
Holt *H. & W.* 52 A5
Holt *Norf.* 23 D2
Holt *Wilts.* 8 B1
Holt *Wrex.* 19 F2
Holt End *H. & W.* 52 C5
Holt Fleet 52 A5
Holt Heath *H. & W.* 52 A5
Holtspur 50 A2
Holy Cross 52 B4
Holyhead 18 A1
Holywell 19 E1
Holywood 29 D1
Homersfield 17 E1
Honiley 53 E4
Honiton 5 E1
Honley 25 F3
Hoo 11 D1
Hook *E.Riding* 26 B3

Hook *Gt.Lon.* 50 C5
Hook *Hants.* 9 F1
Hook Green (Meopham)
Kent 51 H5
Hook Green (Southfleet)
Kent 51 H4
Hook Norton 15 D2
Hope 19 E2
Hopeman 42 B2
Hopton *Norf.* 23 F4
Hopton *Suff.* 17 D1
Hopwas 53 D1
Hopwood 52 C4
Horam 10 C3
Horbling 22 A3
Horbury 26 A3
Horden 31 D2
Horeb 12 B3
Horley 10 B2
Horn Hill 50 B2
Hornby 25 D1
Horncastle 22 A1
Hornchurch 51 G3
Horndean *Hants.* 9 E3
Horndon on the Hill 51 H3
Horning 23 E3
Hornsea 27 D2
Hornsey 51 E3
Horrabridge 4 C2
Horringer 16 C1
Horsehouse 25 F1
Horsford 23 E3
Horsforth 25 F2
Horsham 10 B3
Horsmonden 11 D3
Horstead 23 E3
Horton *Berks.* 50 B4
Horton Heath 9 E3
Horton in Ribblesdale
25 E1
Horton Kirby 51 G5
Horwich 25 D3
Houbie 48 C1
Houghton le Spring 31 D2
Houghton Regis 15 F2
Houndslow 35 D2
Hounslow 50 C4
Houston 33 E2
Houton 49 E3
Hove 10 B4
Hoveton 23 E3
Hovingham 26 B1
Howden 26 B3
Howwood 33 E2
Hoylake 19 E1
Hoyland 26 A4
Hucclecote 14 A3
Hucknall 21 D2
Huddersfield 25 F3
Huggate 26 C2
Huish Episcopi 7 F4
Huisinis 47 D3
Hullavington 14 B4
Hullbridge 11 D1
Humberside International
Airport 27 D3
Humberston 27 E4
Humbie 34 C2
Hundleby 22 B1
Hundleton 12 A2
Hungerford 9 D1
Hunmanby 27 D1
Hunningham 53 F5
Hunstanton 22 C2
Hunt End 52 C5
Hunter's Quay 33 E1
Huntingdon 16 A1
Huntly 43 D3

Huntonbridge 50 B1
Hurley *Warks.* 53 E2
Hurlford 33 F3
Hursley 9 D2
Hurst Green 11 D3
Hurstbourne Tarrant 9 D1
Hurstpierpoint 10 B3
Hurworth-on-Tees 31 D3
Husbands Bosworth 21 E4
Huttoft 22 B1
Hutton *Essex* 51 H2
Hutton Cranswick 27 D2
Hutton Rudby 31 D4
Huyton 19 F1
Hyde 25 E4
Hyde Heath 50 A1
Hythe *Hants.* 9 D3
Hythe *Kent* 11 E3
Hythe End 50 B4

I

Ibstock 21 D3
Ickenham 50 B3
Icklesham 11 D4
Icklingham 16 C1
Idrigil 40 B2
Ifield or Singlewell 51 H4
Ilchester 7 F4
Ilford 10 C1
Ilford 51 F3
Ilfracombe 6 B3
Ilkeston 21 D2
Ilkley 25 F2
Illey 52 B3
Ilminster 7 F4
Immingham 27 D3
Inchbare 39 E2
Inchnadamph 44 B3
Inchture 39 D3
Ingatestone 16 C4
Ingatestone 51 H1
Ingleton *Dur.* 30 C3
Ingleton *N.Yorks.* 25 D1
Inglewhite 25 D2
Ingoldmells 22 B1
Ingrave 51 H2
Inkberrow 14 B1
Innellan 33 D2
Innerleithen 34 C3
Insch 43 D3
Inveralligan 40 C2
Inverallochy 43 F2
Inveraray 37 D3
Inverarity 39 D3
Inverarnan 37 F4
Inverbervie 39 F1
Invercassley 44 C4
Invercharnan 37 E2
Inverey 38 C1
Invergarry 41 E4
Invergordon 42 A2
Inverinan 37 E4
Inverkeilor 39 E2
Inverkeithing 34 B1
Inverkirkaig 44 A3
Inverlael 41 E1
Invermoriston 41 F4
Inverneil 32 C1
Inverness 42 A3
Inverness (Dalcross)
Airport 42 A2
Invernoaden 37 E4
Inverurie 43 E4
Ipplepen 5 D2
Ipstones 20 B2
Ipswich 17 E2
Irchester 15 F1

am 25 D4
onbridge 20 A3
hlingborough 15 F1
vine 33 E3
bister (Mainland) *Shet.*
  48 B1
bister (Whalsay) *Shet.*
  48 C2
e of Man Airport 24 A3
e of Whithorn 28 C2
eham 16 C1
eworth 50 C4
lington 51 E3
ead Rise 51 H5
er 10 A1
er 50 B3
er Heath 50 B3
nghoe 15 F3
ybridge 4 C3
ade 11 D2
worth 17 D1

rrow 31 D1
ywick 17 E3
dburgh 35 D3
mimaville 42 A2
hn o' Groats 45 F1
hnston 12 A2
hnstone 33 E2
hnstonebridge 34 B4
rdans 50 A2

mes 33 D1
arsley 25 D4
dington 16 C2
elby 27 D3
ele 20 A2
gworth 21 D3
ighley 25 F2
illmore 32 C1
iss 45 F1
ith 43 D2
llas *Angus* 39 D3
llas *Moray* 42 C2
lso 35 D3
lty 38 C4
lvedon 17 D3
lvedon Hatch 16 B4
lvedon Hatch 51 G2
mnay 43 E4
mpsey 14 B2
mpston 15 F2
ndal 30 A4
nilworth 14 C1
nilworth 53 E4
nmore 38 B2
nnacraig 32 C2
nnethmont 43 D3
nnington 15 D3
nnoway 39 D4
nsaleyre 40 B2
**nsington & Chelsea
  50 D4**
nsworth 15 F3
ntallen 37 E2
nton *Devon* 5 D2
resley 53 F3
sgrave 17 E2
ssingland 23 F4
ston 51 F5
swick 29 F3
ttering 21 F4
ttlebrook 53 E1

Kettletoft 49 F2
Kettlewell 25 E1
Ketton 21 F3
Kew 50 C4
Kewstoke 7 F2
Keyingham 27 D3
Keymer 10 B4
Keynsham 8 A1
Keyworth 21 E2
Kibworth Harcourt 21 E4
Kidbrooke 51 F4
Kiddemore Green 52 A1
Kidderminster 20 B4
Kidderminster 52 A4
Kidlington 15 D3
Kidsgrove 20 B2
Kidwelly (Cydweli) 6 B1
Kielder 35 D4
Kilberry 32 C2
Kilbirnie 33 E2
Kilburn *Derbys.* 21 D2
Kilcadzow 34 A2
Kilchattan 36 B4
Kilchenzie 32 C3
Kilchiaran 32 A2
Kilchoan 36 C2
Kilchoman 32 A2
Kilchrenan 37 D3
Kilconquhar 39 E4
Kilcreggan 33 E1
Kildonan Lodge 45 D3
Kildrummy 43 D4
Kilfinan 33 D1
Kilgetty 6 A1
Kilham *E.Riding* 27 D1
Kilham *Nhumb.* 35 E3
Kilkhampton 6 A4
Killamarsh 26 A4
Killay 6 C1
Killean 32 C2
Killearn 33 F1
Killichonan 38 A2
Killiecrankie 38 B2
Killin 38 A3
Killinghall 26 A1
Killingworth 31 D1
Killundine 36 C2
Kilmacolm 33 E1
Kilmalieu 37 D2
Kilmaluag 40 B2
Kilmarnock 33 F3
Kilmartin 37 D4
Kilmaurs 33 E3
Kilmelford 37 D4
Kilmington 5 F1
Kilmory *Arg. & B.* 32 C1
Kilmory (Rum) *High.* 40 A4
Kilninian 36 B2
Kilninver 37 D3
Kiloran 36 B4
Kilrenny 39 E4
Kilsyth 33 F1
Kilwinning 33 E2
Kimberley *Norf.* 23 D4
Kimberley *Notts.* 21 D2
Kimbolton 16 A1
Kimpton 16 A3
Kinbrace 45 D3
Kincardine 34 A1
Kincardine O'Neil 43 D4
Kincraig 42 A4
Kineton Green 53 D3
Kingarth 33 D2
Kinghorn 34 B1
Kinglassie 39 D4
King's Heath 52 C3
King's Hill 52 B2

Kings Langley 15 F3
Kings Langley 50 B1
King's Lynn 22 C3
**King's Norton W.Mid.
  52 C4**
King's Sutton 15 D2
King's Worthy 9 E2
Kingsbarns 39 E4
Kingsbridge 4 C3
Kingsbury Gt.Lon. 50 C3
Kingsbury *Warks.* 20 C4
Kingsbury Warks. 53 E2
Kingsbury Episcopi 7 F4
Kingsclere 9 E1
Kingsdown 11 F2
Kingsford H. & W. 52 A3
Kingshouse 38 A3
Kingskerswell 5 D3
Kingsley *Ches.* 19 F1
Kingsley *Staffs.* 20 B2
Kingsnorth 11 E3
Kingstanding 52 C2
Kingsteignton 5 D2
Kingsthorne 13 F4
Kingston 42 C2
Kingston Bagpuize 15 D3
Kingston Seymour 7 F2
Kingston upon Hull 27 D3
**Kingston upon Thames
  50 C4**
Kingstone 13 F4
Kingswear 5 D3
Kingswinford 52 A3
Kingswood *S.Glos.* 14 A4
Kingswood *Surr.* 10 B2
Kingswood Warks. 53 D4
Kington 13 E3
Kingussie 42 A4
Kinloch 40 B4
Kinloch Hourn 41 D4
Kinloch Rannoch 38 A2
Kinlochard 38 A4
Kinlochbervie 44 B2
Kinlocheil 37 E1
Kinlochewe 41 D2
Kinlochleven 37 E2
Kinloss 42 B2
Kinmel Bay 19 D1
Kinross 38 C4
Kintbury 9 D1
Kintore 43 E4
Kintour 32 B2
Kintra 32 A2
Kinver 20 B4
Kinver 52 A3
Kippax 26 A3
Kippen 38 A4
Kirby Corner 53 E4
Kirby Muxloe 21 D3
Kirk Michael 24 A2
Kirk Sandall 26 B3
Kirk Yetholm 35 E3
Kirkbean 29 D2
Kirkbride 29 E2
Kirkburton 25 F3
Kirkby *Mersey.* 24 C4
Kirkby in Ashfield 21 D1
Kirkby Lonsdale 25 D1
Kirkby Malzeard 25 F1
Kirkby Stephen 30 B4
Kirkbymoorside 31 E4
Kirkcaldy 34 B1
Kirkcolm 28 A1
Kirkconnel 34 A4
Kirkcowan 28 B2
Kirkcudbright 28 C2
Kirkham 24 C2

Kirkinner 28 B2
Kirkintilloch 33 F1
Kirkliston 34 B1
Kirkmichael *P. & K.* 38 C2
Kirkmichael *S.Ayr.* 33 E4
Kirkmuirhill 34 A2
Kirknewton *Nhumb.* 35 E3
Kirknewton *W.Loth.* 34 B2
Kirkoswald *Cumb.* 30 A2
Kirkoswald *S.Ayr.* 33 E4
Kirkpatrick Durham 29 D1
Kirkpatrick-Fleming 29 F1
Kirkton 37 D4
Kirkton of Culsalmond
  43 D3
Kirkton of Durris 39 F1
Kirkton of Glenisla 39 D2
Kirkton of Kingoldrum
  39 D2
Kirkton of Menmuir 39 E2
Kirkton of Skene 43 E4
Kirktown of Auchterless
  43 E3
Kirktown of Deskford
  43 D2
Kirkwall 49 E3
Kirmington 15 D3
Kirriemuir 39 D2
Kirtlington 15 D3
Kirton *Lincs.* 22 A2
Kirton *Suff.* 17 E2
Kirton in Lindsey 26 C4
Knaresborough 26 A2
Knayton 31 D4
Knebworth 16 A3
Knighton 13 E2
Knock 36 C3
Knockandhu 42 C4
Knottingley 26 A3
Knotty Green 50 A2
Knowle *W.Mid.* 20 C4
Knowle W.Mid. 53 D4
Knucklas 13 E2
Knutsford 20 A1
Kyle of Lochalsh 40 C3
Kyleakin 40 C3
Kylerhea 40 C4
Kylestrome 44 B2

L
Laceby 27 D4
Lacock 8 B1
Ladybank 39 D4
Ladykirk 35 E2
Ladysford 43 E2
Lagg 33 D3
Laggan (Invergarry) *High.*
  37 F1
Laggan (Newtonmore)
  High. 38 A1
Lagganulva 36 C3
Laide 41 D1
Laindon 51 H3
Lairg 44 C2
Lakenheath 16 C1
Laleham 50 B5
Laleston 7 D2
Lamberhurst 11 D3
Lambeth 50 D4
Lambourn 15 D4
Lambourne End 51 F2
Lamlash 33 D3
Lampeter 12 C3
Lamport 15 E1
Lanark 34 A2
Lancaster 24 C1
Lanchester 30 C2

Landore 6 C1
Landywood 52 B1
Lane End *Bucks.* 15 E4
Lane End Kent 51 G4
Lane Green 52 A1
Langdon Hills 51 H3
Langford 16 A2
Langham 21 F3
Langholm 29 F1
Langley Berks. 50 B4
Langley Warks. 53 D5
Langold 26 B4
Langport 7 F4
Langtoft 26 C1
Langwathby 30 A3
Lanivet 4 A2
Lanton 14 C1
Lapworth 53 D4
Larbert 34 A1
Largoward 39 D4
Largs 33 E2
Larkhall 34 A2
Larkhill 8 C1
Larling 23 D4
Latchingdon 17 D4
Latheron 45 E2
Latheronwheel 45 E3
Latimer 50 B2
Lauder 34 C2
Laugharne 6 B1
Launceston 4 B1
Laurencekirk 39 E2
Laurieston 28 C1
Lavenham 17 D2
Law 34 A2
Lawers 38 A3
Lawford 17 D3
Laxey 24 B2
Laxford Bridge 44 B2
Laxo 48 B2
Layer de la Haye 17 D3
Lazonby 30 A2
Lea Marston 53 E2
Leadburn 34 B2
Leadenham 21 F2
Leadgate 30 C2
Leadhills 34 A3
Leasingham 21 F2
Leatherhead 10 A2
Leavening 26 C1
Leaves Green 51 F5
Lechlade 14 C3
Leckhampton 14 B3
Leckmelm 41 E1
Ledaig 37 D3
Ledbury 14 A2
Ledmore 44 B3
Lee *Lancs.* 25 D2
Lee Moor 4 C2
Lee-on-the-Solent 9 E3
Leeds *W.Yorks.* 26 A2
Leeds Bradford International
  Airport 25 F2
Leedstown 3 E3
Leek 20 B1
Leek Wootton 53 E5
Leeming 31 D4
Leicester 21 E3
Leigh *Gt.Man.* 25 D4
Leighton Buzzard 15 F2
Leiston 17 F1
Leith 34 B1
Lenham 11 D2
Lennoxtown 33 F1
Leominster 13 F3
Lerwick 48 B3
Lesbury 35 F4

Leslie 39 D4
Lesmahagow 34 A3
Leswalt 28 A1
Letchmore Heath 50 **C2**
Letchworth 16 A2
Letheringsett 23 D2
Letterston 12 B1
Leuchars 39 D3
Leumrabhagh 47 E3
Leven *E.Riding* 27 D2
Leven *Fife* 39 D4
Levenwick 48 B4
Leverstock Green 50 **B1**
Lewes 10 B4
Lewisham 51 E4
Leyburn 30 C4
Leyland 25 D3
Leysdown-on-Sea 11 E1
Leyton 51 E3
Lhanbryde 42 C2
Libberton 34 A2
Lichfield 20 C3
Lichfield 53 D1
Lickey 52 B4
Lickey End 52 B4
Lightwater 9 F1
Lightwater 50 A5
Lilleshall 20 A3
Lilliesleaf 34 C3
Limekilns 34 B1
Lincoln 21 F1
Lincomb 52 A5
Lindfield 10 B3
Lindores 39 D4
Linford *Essex* 11 D1
Linford *Essex* 51 H4
Lingfield 10 B2
Linksness 49 D3
Linlithgow 34 A1
Linsidemore 41 F1
Linton 16 B2
Liphook 9 F2
Liskeard 4 B2
Liss 9 F2
Liswerry 7 F2
Litherland 24 C4
Little Aston 52 C2
Little Berkhamsted
  50 D1
Little Burstead 51 H2
Little Chalfont 50 A2
Little Clacton 17 E3
Little Common 11 D4
Little Downham 16 B1
Little Eaton 21 D2
Little End 51 G1
Little Hay 53 D1
Little Heath 53 F3
Little Laver 51 G1
Little Missenden 15 F3
Little Missenden 50 A2
Little Oakley 17 E3
Little Parndon 51 F1
Little Paxton 16 A1
Little Plumstead 23 E3
Little Thurrock 51 H4
Little Warley 51 H2
Little Wyrley 52 C1
Littleborough 25 E3
Littlebourne 11 F2
Littledean 14 A3
Littlehampton 10 A4
Littlemill *E.Ayr.* 33 F4
Littlemill *High.* 42 B2
Littlemore 15 D3
Littleport 22 B4
Littlestone-on-Sea 11 E3

Littleton *Surr.* **50 B5**
Liverpool 19 E1
Liversedge 25 F3
Livingston 34 B1
Lizard 3 E4
Llanaelhaearn 18 B2
Llanarth 12 B3
Llanarthney 12 B4
Llanbadarn Fawr 12 C2
Llanbadrig 18 A1
Llanbedr 18 B3
Llanbedrog 18 A3
Llanberis 18 B2
Llanbister 13 E2
Llanblethian 7 D2
Llanddarog 12 B4
Llanddeiniolen 18 B2
Llandderfel 19 D3
Llanddowror 6 A1
Llandeilo 12 C4
Llandinam 13 D2
Llandissilio 12 A4
Llandovery 12 C4
Llandrillo 19 D3
Llandrindod Wells 13 E3
Llandudno 18 C1
Llandwrog 18 B2
Llandybie 12 C4
Llandysul 12 B4
Llanegwad 12 B4
Llanelli 6 B1
Llanelltyd 18 C3
Llanelly 13 E4
Llanelwy (St. Asaph)
  19 D1
Llanerchymedd 18 B1
Llanfaelog 18 A1
Llanfair Caereinion 13 E1
Llanfair Talhaiarn 19 D1
Llanfairfechan 18 C1
Llanfairpwllgwyngyll
  18 B1
Llanfihangel ar-arth 12 B4
Llanfyllin 19 D3
Llanfynydd 19 E2
Llangadfan 13 D1
Llangadog 12 C4
Llangefni 18 B1
Llangeler 12 B4
Llangelynin 12 C1
Llangendeirne 6 B1
Llangernyw 18 C2
Llangoed 18 B1
Llangollen 19 E3
Llangranog 12 B3
Llangunnor 12 B4
Llangurig 13 D2
Llangwm 12 B2
Llangynidr 13 E4
Llanharan 7 D2
Llanhilleth 7 E1
Llanidloes 13 D2
Llanilar 12 C2
Llanishen *Cardiff* 7 E2
Llanllwchaiarn 13 E2
Llanllyfni 18 B2
Llannon 6 B1
Llanon 12 B3
Llanrhaeadr-ym-Mochnant
  19 D3
Llanrhidian 6 B1
Llanrhystud 12 B2
Llanrug 18 B2
Llanrumney 7 E2
Llanrwst 18 C2
Llansamlet 6 C1
Llansannan 19 D2

Llansantffraid Glan Conwy
  18 C1
Llansawel 12 C4
Llanstephan 6 B1
Llanthony 13 E4
Llantilio Pertholey 13 F4
Llantrisant *Mon.* 7 F1
Llantrisant *R.C.T.* 7 D2
Llantwit Major 7 D2
Llanuwchllyn 18 C3
Llanwddyn 19 D3
Llanwnda 18 B2
Llanwnog 13 D1
Llanwrda 12 C4
Llanwrtyd Wells 13 D3
Llanybydder 12 B3
Llanynghenedl 18 A1
Llanystumdwy 18 B3
Lledrod 12 C2
Loanhead 34 B2
Loans 33 E3
Loch Baghasdail
  (Lochboisdale) 46 B3
Loch na Madadh
  (Lochmaddy) 46 B1
Loch Sgioport 46 B2
Lochailort 37 D1
Lochaline 36 C3
Lochans 28 A2
Locharbriggs 29 E1
Lochawe 37 E3
Lochboisdale (Loch
  Baghasdail) 46 B3
Lochcarron 41 D3
Lochdon 37 D3
Lochearnhead 38 A3
Lochend 41 F3
Lochgelly 38 C4
Lochgilphead 32 C1
Lochgoilhead 37 F4
Lochinver 44 A3
Lochmaben 29 E1
Lochmaddy (Loch na
  Madadh) 46 B1
Lochranza 33 D2
Lochwinnoch 33 E2
Lockerbie 29 E1
Locking 7 F3
Locks Heath 9 E3
Locksbottom 51 F5
Lockton 31 F4
Loddiswell 4 C3
Loddon 23 E3
Lofthouse *W.Yorks.* 26 A3
Loftus 31 E3
Logan 33 F3
Loggerheads 20 A2
London 10 B3
London City Airport 51 F3
London Colney 16 A4
London Colney 50 C1
Long Ashton 7 F2
Long Bennington 21 F2
Long Buckby 15 E1
Long Compton 14 C2
Long Crendon 15 E3
Long Ditton 50 C5
Long Eaton 21 D2
Long Hanborough 15 D3
Long Itchington 15 D1
Long Lawford 21 D4
Long Melford 17 D2
Long Preston 25 E1
Long Stratton 23 E4
Long Sutton *Lincs.* 22 B3
Long Sutton *Som.* 7 F4
Longbenton 31 D1

Longbridge *Warks.*
  53 E5
Longbridge *W.Mid.*
  52 C4
Longbridge Deverill 8 B2
Longcross *Surr.* **50 A5**
Longdon 20 C3
Longfield 51 H5
Longfield Hill 51 H5
Longford *Gt.Lon.* **50 B4**
Longford *W.Mid.* **53 F3**
Longforgan 39 D3
Longframlington 35 F4
Longhope *Glos.* 14 A3
Longhope *Ork.* 49 D4
Longhorsley 35 F4
Longhoughton 35 F3
Longmanhill 43 E2
Longmorn 42 C2
Longniddry 34 C1
Longridge 25 D2
Longside 43 F3
Longton *Lancs.* 24 C3
Longtown 29 F1
Looe 4 B3
Loose 11 D2
Lopcombe Corner 9 D2
Loscoe 21 D2
Lossiemouth 42 C2
Lostwithiel 4 A2
Loth 49 F2
Lothmore 45 E3
Loughborough 21 D3
Loughor 6 C1
Loughton *Essex* 16 B4
Loughton *Essex* **51 F2**
Louth 22 A1
Loves Green 51 H1
Low Habberley 52 A4
Low Street 23 E3
Lowdham 21 E2
Lower Beeding 10 B3
Lower Cam 14 A3
Lower Diabaig 40 C2
Lower Green *Staffs.*
  52 B1
Lower Killeyan 32 A3
Lower Nazeing 51 E1
Lower Penn 52 A2
Lowestoft 23 F4
Loweswater 29 E3
Lowick 35 E3
Lowsonford 53 D5
Ludag 46 A3
Luddesdown 51 H5
Ludgershall 9 D1
Ludgvan 3 D3
Ludlow 13 F2
Luib 40 B3
Lumphanan 43 D4
Luncarty 38 C3
Lundin Links 39 D4
Luss 33 E1
Lusta 40 A2
Luton 16 A3
Luton (London) Airport
  16 A3
Lutterworth 21 D4
Luxulyan 4 A3
Lybster 45 F2
Lydd 11 E3
Lydford 4 C1
Lydiate 24 C4
Lydney 14 A3
Lye 52 B3
Lye Green 50 A1
Lyme Regis 5 F1

Lyminge 11 E3
Lymington 9 D3
Lymm 25 D4
Lympne 11 E3
Lympstone 5 D2
Lyndhurst 9 D3
Lyne *Surr.* **50 B5**
Lyne of Skene 43 E4
Lyneham 14 B4
Lynemore 42 B3
Lynemouth 35 F4
Lyness 49 D4
Lynmouth 6 C3
Lynton 6 C3
Lytchett Matravers 8 B3
Lytchett Minster 8 C3
Lytham St. Anne's 24 C3

M

Mablethorpe 22 B1
Macclesfield 20 B1
Macduff 43 E2
Macharioch 32 C4
Machen 7 E1
Machrihanish 32 B3
Machynlleth 12 C1
Macmerry 34 C1
Madeley *Staffs.* 20 A2
Madley 13 F4
Madron 3 D3
Maenclochog 12 A4
Maentwrog 18 C3
Maerdy 7 D1
Maesteg 7 D1
Magdalen Laver 51 G1
Maghull 24 C4
Maiden Bradley 8 B2
Maiden Newton 8 A3
Maidenhead 15 F4
Maidens 33 E4
Maidstone 11 D2
Malden 50 D5
Malden Rushett 50 C5
Maldon 17 D4
Mallaig 36 C1
Mallwyd 13 D1
Malmesbury 14 B4
Malpas 7 F1
Malpas *Ches.* 19 F2
Maltby *S.Yorks.* 26 B4
Maltby le Marsh 22 B1
Malton 26 C1
Malvern Link 14 A2
Manby 22 B1
Mancetter 20 C4
Mancetter 53 F2
Manchester 25 E4
Manchester Airport 25 E4
Manea 22 B4
Mangotsfield 14 A4
Manningtree 17 E3
Manorbier 6 A1
Mansfield 21 D1
Mansfield Woodhouse
  21 D1
Manston 8 B3
Maple Cross 50 B2
Mappleborough Green
  52 C5
Marazion 3 E3
March 22 B4
Marchwiel 19 E2
Marden *Kent* 11 D2
Mareham le Fen 22 A2
Maresfield 10 C3
Margam 6 C2

Margaretting 51 H1
Margate 11 F1
Marham 22 C3
Mark 7 F3
Market Bosworth 21 D3
Market Deeping 22 A3
Market Drayton 20 A2
Market Harborough 21 E4
Market Lavington 8 C1
Market Rasen 27 D4
Market Weighton 26 C2
Markfield 21 D3
Markinch 39 D4
Marks Gate 51 F3
Marks Tey 17 D3
Markyate 15 F3
Marlborough 8 C1
Marldon 5 D2
Marlow 15 F4
Marnhull 8 B2
Marple 25 E4
Marsden *W.Yorks.* 25 F3
Marshfield *S.Glos.* 14 A4
Marske-by-the-Sea 31 E3
Marston *Oxon.* 15 D3
Marston *Warks.* 53 E2
Marston Green 53 D3
Marston Magna 8 A2
Marston Moretaine 15 F2
Martham 23 F3
Martlesham 17 E2
Martley 14 A1
Martock 7 F4
Marybank 41 F2
Marykirk 39 E2
Marylebone *Gt.Lon.* 50 D3
Marypark 42 C3
Maryport 29 E2
Marywell 39 E1
Masham 25 F1
Matlock 20 C1
Matlock Bath 20 C1
Mauchline 33 F3
Maud 43 F3
Maughold 24 B2
Maw Green 52 C2
Maxstoke 53 E3
Maybole 33 E4
Mayfield 20 C2
Mealsgate 29 E2
Meare 7 F3
Measham 21 D3
Medstead 9 E2
Meer End 53 E4
Meidrim 12 A4
Meigle 39 D3
Meikle Kilmory 33 D2
Meikleour 38 C3
Melbourn 16 B2
Melbourne 21 D3
Melksham 8 B1
Melmerby 30 A2
Melrose 34 C3
Melsonby 30 C4
Meltham 25 F3
Melton 17 E2
Melton Mowbray 21 E3
Melvaig 40 C1
Melvich 45 D1
Memsie 43 F2
Menai Bridge 18 B1
Menston 25 F2
Menstrie 38 B4
Meopham 51 H5
Meopham Green 51 H5
Mere *Wilts.* 8 B2
Mere Green 53 D2

Meriden 20 C4
Meriden 53 E3
Merry Hill 50 C2
Merthyr Tydfil 7 D1
Merton *Gt.Lon.* 50 D5
Messingham 26 C4
Metfield 17 E1
Metheringham 21 F1
Methlick 43 E3
Methven 38 C3
Methwold 22 C4
Mevagissey 4 A3
Mexborough 26 A4
Mey 45 F1
Miabhig 47 D2
Mickleton *Dur.* 30 B3
Mickleton *Glos.* 14 C2
Mid Ardlaw 43 F2
Mid Yell 48 C1
Midbea 49 E2
Middle Barton 15 D2
Middle Rasen 27 D4
Middleham 30 C4
Middlemarsh 8 A3
Middlesbrough 31 D3
Middlesmoor 25 F1
Middleton *Gt.Man.* 25 E4
Middleton *Norf.* 22 C4
Middleton *Warks.* 53 D2
Middleton Cheney 15 D2
Middleton Stoney 15 D3
Middleton-in-Teesdale
30 B3
Middleton-on-Sea 10 A4
Middleton-on-the-Wolds
26 C2
Middlewich 20 A1
Midhurst 9 F2
Midlem 34 C3
Midsomer Norton 8 A1
Milborne Port 8 A2
Milborne St. Andrew 8 B3
Mildenhall 16 C1
Mile End 17 D3
Milfield 35 E3
Milford *Surr.* 9 F2
Milford Haven 12 A2
Milford on Sea 9 D4
Mill Green Essex 51 H1
Mill Hill 50 D2
Millbrook *Cornw.* 4 B3
Millhouse 33 D1
Millom 24 B1
Millport 33 D2
Milltown of Rothiemay
43 D3
Milnathort 38 C4
Milngavie 33 F1
Milnrow 25 E3
Milnthorpe 24 C1
Milovaig 40 A2
Milton *High.* 41 F3
Milton *P. & K.* 38 B3
Milton Keynes 15 F2
Milton of Campsie 33 F1
Milverton 7 E4
Minard 37 E4
Minchinhampton 14 B3
Minehead 7 D3
Minera 19 E2
Minnigaff 28 B1
Minster (Sheppey) *Kent*
11 E1
Minster (Thanet) *Kent*
11 F2
Minsterley 13 F1
Mintlaw 43 F3

Minworth 53 D2
Mirfield 25 F3
Misterton 26 B4
Mitcham 50 D5
Mitcheldean 14 A3
Mobberley 20 A1
Modbury 4 C3
Moelfre 18 B1
Moffat 34 B4
Mold 19 E2
Molescroft 27 D2
Moniaive 34 A4
Monifieth 39 E3
Monimail 39 D4
Monken Hadley 50 D2
Monkokehampton 4 C1
Monks Eleigh 17 D2
Monmore Green 52 B2
Monmouth (Trefynwy) 7 F1
Monreith 28 B2
Montgomery (Trefaldwyn)
13 E1
Montrose 39 E2
Moorends 26 B3
Morar 36 C1
Morden *Gt.Lon.* 50 D5
Morebattle 35 D3
Morecambe 24 C1
Morenish 38 A3
Moresby 29 E3
Moreton Essex 51 G1
Moreton *Mersey.* 19 E1
Moreton-in-Marsh 14 C2
Moretonhampstead 5 D1
Morfa Nefyn 18 A3
Morley *W.Yorks.* 26 A3
Morpeth 30 C1
Morriston 6 C1
Mortehoe 6 B3
Mortimer's Cross 13 F3
Mortlake 50 D4
Morton (Bourne) *Lincs.*
22 A3
Morton (Gainsborough)
Lincs. 26 C4
Morton Bagot 53 D5
Morville 20 A4
Mosborough 26 A4
Moscow 33 F3
Moseley *W.Mid.* 52 C3
Mossat 43 D4
Mossblown 33 E3
Mossley 25 E4
Mosstodloch 42 C2
Motherwell 34 A2
Mottingham 51 F4
Moulsecoomb 10 B4
Moulton *Lincs.* 22 B3
Moulton *Suff.* 16 C1
Mountain Ash 7 E1
Mountbenger 34 C3
Mountnessing 51 H2
Mountsorrel 21 E3
Moxley 52 B2
Moy 42 A3
Much Wenlock 20 A4
Muchalls 39 F1
Muir of Fowlis 43 D4
Muir of Ord 41 F2
Muirdrum 39 E3
Muirhead *Angus*
39 D3
Muirkirk 33 F3
Mulbarton 23 E4
Mulben 42 C2
Mullion 3 E4
Mundesley 23 E2

Mundford 22 C4
Munlochy 42 A2
Murton 31 D2
Musbury 5 F1
Musselburgh 34 C1
Mustow Green 52 A4
Muthill 38 B4
Mybster 45 E2
Mytholmroyd 25 E3

N

Nailsea 7 F2
Nailsworth 14 B3
Nairn 42 A2
Nantwich 20 A2
Nantyglo 7 E1
Narberth 6 A1
Narborough *Leics.* 21 D4
Narborough *Norf.* 22 C3
Nateby 30 B4
Navestock 51 G2
Navestock Side 51 G2
Nazeing 16 B4
Nazeing 51 F1
Neal's Green 53 F3
Near Sawrey 29 F4
Neath 6 C1
Necton 23 D4
Needham Market 17 D2
Needingworth 16 B1
Nefyn 18 A3
Neilston 33 F2
Nelson 25 E2
Nenthead 30 B2
Neston 19 E1
Nether Langwith 21 D1
Nether Stowey 7 E3
Nether Whitacre 53 E2
Netherley 39 F1
Netherton *Nhumb.* 35 E4
**Netherton *W.Mid.*
52 B3**
Nethy Bridge 42 B4
Nettlebed 15 E4
Nettleham 21 F1
New Abbey 29 D1
New Aberdour 43 E2
New Addington 10 B2
New Addington 51 E5
New Alresford 9 E2
New Arley 53 E2
New Ash Green 10 C2
New Ash Green 51 H5
New Barn 51 H5
New Barnet 50 D2
New Byth 43 E2
New Cumnock 33 F4
New Deer 43 E3
New Eltham 51 F4
New Galloway 28 C1
New Haw 50 B5
**New Invention *W.Mid.*
52 B1**
New Leeds 43 F2
New Luce 28 A1
New Malden 50 D5
New Mills 25 E4
New Milton 9 D3
New Mistley 17 E3
New Pitsligo 43 E2
New Quay 12 B3
New Radnor 13 E3
New Romney 11 E3
New Rossington 26 B4
New Scone 38 C3
New Tredegar 7 E1
Newark-on-Trent 21 E1

Newbiggin-by-the-Sea
31 D1
Newbigging 34 A2
Newbold Verdon 21 D3
Newborough 22 A4
Newbridge *Caerp.* 7 E1
Newburgh *Aber.* 43 F3
Newburgh *Fife* 39 D4
Newburn 30 C1
Newbury 9 E1
Newby Bridge 29 F4
Newcastle *Shrop.* 13 E2
Newcastle Airport 30 C1
Newcastle Emlyn 12 B4
Newcastle upon Tyne
30 C1
Newcastle-under-Lyme
20 B2
Newcastleton 29 F1
Newent 14 A2
Newgate Street 51 E1
Newham *Gt.Lon.* 51 E3
Newhaven 10 C4
Newick 10 B3
Newington 11 D2
Newlyn 3 D3
Newmachar 43 E4
Newmains 34 A2
Newmarket *Suff.* 16 C1
Newmarket *W.Isles* 47 F2
Newmill 43 D2
Newmilns 33 F3
Newnham 14 A3
Newport *Essex* 16 B2
Newport *High.* 45 E3
Newport *I.o.W.* 9 E4
Newport *Newport* 7 F2
Newport *Pembs.* 12 A4
Newport *Shrop.* 20 A3
Newport Pagnell 15 F2
Newport-on-Tay 39 D3
Newquay 3 F2
Newton *Arg. & B.* 37 E4
Newton (Bowland) *Lancs.*
25 D2
Newton Abbot 5 D2
Newton Aycliffe 31 D3
Newton Burgoland 53 F1
Newton Ferrers 4 C3
Newton Mearns 33 F2
Newton Poppleford 5 E1
Newton Regis 53 E1
Newton St. Cyres 5 D1
Newton Stewart 28 B1
Newton-le-Willows
Mersey. 19 F1
Newtonhill 39 F1
Newtonmore 42 A4
Newtown *Bucks.* 50 A1
Newtown *H. & W.* 14 A2
Newtown (Y Drenewydd)
Powys 13 E2
Newtown St. Boswells
35 D3
Newtyle 39 D3
Neyland 12 B2
Nine Ashes 51 G1
Ninemile Bar or
Crocketford 29 D1
Ninfield 11 D4
Nisbet 35 D3
**No Man's Heath *Warks.*
53 E1**
Noak Hill 51 G2
Norbiton 50 C5
Norchard 52 A5
Norham 35 E2

Normanton *W.Yorks.*
26 A3
North Baddesley 9 D2
North Ballachulish 37 E2
North Berwick 34 C1
North Cave 26 C2
North Cheriton 8 A2
North Cowton 31 D4
North Cray 51 F4
North Duffield 26 B2
North Elmham 23 D3
North Ferriby 26 C3
North Grimston 26 C1
North Hykeham 21 F1
North Leigh 15 D3
North Middleton 34 C2
North Molton 6 C4
North Ockendon 51 G3
North Queensferry 34 B1
North Shields 31 D1
North Somercotes 27 E4
North Stifford 51 H3
North Sunderland 35 F3
North Thoresby 27 E4
North Tidworth 9 D1
North Walsham 23 E3
North Weald Bassett
16 B4
**North Weald Bassett
51 F1**
North Wingfield 21 D1
Northam *Devon* 6 B4
Northampton 15 E1
Northaw 50 D1
Northchurch 50 A1
Northfield *W.Mid.* 52 C4
Northfleet 10 C1
Northfleet 51 H4
Northill 16 A2
Northleach 14 C3
Northolt 50 C3
Northwich 20 A1
Northwood *Gt.Lon.* 50 B2
Northwood *I.o.W.* 9 E3
Norton *N.Yorks.* 26 C1
Norton *Suff.* 17 D1
Norton *W.Mid.* 52 A3
Norton Canes 20 B3
Norton Canes 52 C1
Norton Fitzwarren 7 E4
Norton Heath 51 H1
Norton Lindsey 53 E5
Norton Mandeville 51 G1
**Norton-Juxta-Twycross
53 F1**
Norwich 23 E4
Norwich Airport 23 E3
Norwick 48 C1
Norwood Green 50 C4
Nottingham 21 D2
Nuneaton 21 D4
Nuneaton 53 F2
Nurton 52 A2
Nuthurst *Warks.* 53 D4

O
Oadby 21 E4
Oakdale 7 E1
Oaken 52 A1
Oakengates 20 A3
Oakham 21 F3
Oakley *Bucks.* 15 E3
Oakley *Fife* 34 A1
Oakley *Hants.* 9 E1

Oakley Green 50 A4
Oban 37 D3
Ochiltree 33 F3
Ockbrook 21 D2
Ockle 36 C2
Oddsta 48 C1
Odiham 9 F1
Odstone 53 F1
Offchurch 53 F5
Ogmore 7 D2
Ogmore Vale 7 D1
Okehampton 4 C1
Old Arley 53 E2
Old Colwyn 18 C1
Old Dailly 33 E4
Old Felixstowe 17 E2
Old Hill 52 B3
Old Leake 22 B2
Old Milverton 53 E5
Old Swinford 52 B3
Old Town 25 D1
Old Windsor 50 A4
Oldberrow 53 D5
Oldbury *Warks.* 53 F2
Oldbury *W.Mid.* 20 B4
Oldbury *W.Mid.* 52 B2
Oldfield *H. & W.* 52 A5
Oldham 25 E4
Oldland 8 A1
Oldmeldrum 43 E3
Olgrinmore 45 E2
Ollaberry 48 B2
Ollerton *Notts.* 21 E1
Olney 15 F1
Olton 53 D3
Olveston 14 A4
Ombersley 14 A1
Ombersley 52 A5
Onchan 24 B3
Onich 37 E2
Orford *Suff.* 17 F2
Ormesby St. Margaret
23 F3
Ormiston 34 C1
Ormskirk 24 C3
Orpington 10 C2
Orpington 51 F5
Orrell 25 D3
Orsett 51 H3
Orton 30 A4
Orton Longueville 22 A4
Orton-on-the-Hill 53 F1
Oskaig 40 B3
Ossett 26 A3
Osterley 50 C4
Oswaldkirk 26 B1
Oswaldtwistle 25 D3
Oswestry 19 E3
Otford 10 C2
Otley *Suff.* 17 E2
Otley *W.Yorks.* 25 F2
Otter Ferry 33 D1
Otterburn 35 E4
Ottershaw 50 B5
Otterswick 48 C2
Ottery St. Mary 5 E1
Oughtibridge 26 A4
Oulton *Suff.* 23 F4
Oundle 21 F4
Outwell 22 B4
Over Wallop 9 D2
Over Whitacre 53 E2
Overbister 49 F2
Overseal 20 C3
Overton *Hants.* 9 E1
Overton *Wrex.* 19 E3
Overtown 34 A2

Oxenhope 25 F2
Oxford 15 D3
Oxley 52 B1
Oxnam 35 D3
Oxshott 10 A2
Oxshott 50 C5
Oxted 10 B2
Oxton *Sc.Bord.* 34 C2
Oykel Bridge 41 F1

P
Padbury 15 E2
Paddington 50 D3
Paddock Wood 11 D2
Padiham 25 E2
Padstow 3 F2
Paignton 5 D2
Painswick 14 B3
Paisley 33 F2
Palnackie 29 D2
Pandy 13 F4
Pangbourne 15 E4
Pant-y-dwr 13 D2
Papworth Everard 16 A1
Par 4 A3
Parbold 24 C3
Parkgate 29 E1
Partney 22 B1
Parton 29 D3
Passingford Bridge 51 F2
Patchway 14 A4
Pateley Bridge 25 F1
Path of Condie 38 C4
Patna 33 E4
Patrick 24 A2
Patrington 27 E3
Patterdale 29 F3
Paulton 8 A1
Paxton 35 E2
Peacehaven 10 B4
Peasedown St. John 8 B1
Pedmore 52 B3
Peebles 34 B2
Peel 24 A2
Pegswood 30 C1
Peinchorran 40 B3
Pelsall 20 B3
Pelsall 52 C1
Pelynt 4 A3
Pembrey 6 B1
Pembridge 13 F3
Pembroke 12 B2
Pembroke Dock 12 B2
Pembury 10 C3
Pen-y-bont-fawr 19 D3
Penally 6 A1
Penarth 7 E2
Pencader 12 B4
Pencaitland 34 C1
Pencoed 7 D2
Pendeen 3 D3
Pendine 6 A1
Pendlebury 25 E4
Penge 51 E4
Penicuik 34 B2
Peninver 32 C3
Penistone 25 F4
Penkridge 20 B3
Penley 19 F3
Penmaenmawr 18 C1
Penn *Bucks.* 50 A2
Penn *W.Mid.* 52 A2
Penn Street 50 A2

Pennyghael 36 C3
Penpont 34 A4
Penrhiw-pal 12 B3
Penrhyn Bay 18 C1
Penrhyndeudraeth 18 B3
Penrith 30 A3
Penryn 3 F3
Pensilva 4 B2
Pensnett 52 B3
Pentir 18 B2
Pentraeth 18 B1
Pentre 7 D1
Pentrefoelas 18 C2
Penwortham 25 D3
Penybont 13 E3
Penygraig 7 D1
Penygroes 18 B2
Penywaun 7 D1
Penzance 3 D3
Perivale 50 C3
Perranporth 3 E2
Perry Barr 52 C2
Perry Street 51 H4
Pershore 14 B2
Perth 38 C3
Perton 52 A2
Peterborough 22 A4
Peterculter 43 E4
Peterhead 43 F3
Peterlee 31 D2
Petersfield 9 F2
Petworth 10 A3
Pevensey 10 C4
Pewsey 8 C1
Piccotts End 50 B1
Pickering 31 H4
Pickford Green 53 E3
Piddletrenthide 8 B3
Pierowall 49 E2
Pilgrims Hatch 16 B4
Pilgrims Hatch 51 G2
Pilling 24 C2
Pilning 7 F2
Pimperne 8 B3
Pinchbeck 22 A3
Pinhoe 5 D1
Pinley Green 53 E5
Pinner 50 C2
Pinner Green 50 C2
Pinwherry 28 A1
Pirbright 9 F1
Pirnmill 32 C2
Pitagowan 38 B2
Pitlochry 38 B2
Pitmedden 43 E3
Pitscottie 39 D4
Pitt 9 D2
Pittentrail 42 A1
Pittenweem 39 E4
Plean 34 A1
Pleasley 21 D1
Plumstead *Gt.Lon.* 51 F4
Plwmp 12 B3
Plymouth 4 C3
Plymouth City Airport 4 C2
Plympton 4 C3
Plymstock 4 C3
Pocklington 26 C2
Polbeth 34 A2
Polegate 10 C4
Polesworth 20 C3
Polesworth 53 F1
Pollock 37 D2
Polmont 34 A1
Polperro 4 A3
Polwarth 35 D2

Ponders End 51 E2
Pondersbridge 22 A4
Pontardawe 6 C1
Pontardulais 6 C1
Pontefract 26 A3
Ponteland 30 C1
Pontesbury 13 F1
Pontllanfraith 7 E1
Pontrhydfendigaid 12 C3
Pontrilas 13 F4
Pontyberem 6 B1
Pontycymer 7 D1
Pontypool 7 E1
Pontypridd 7 E1
Pool 25 F2
Poole 8 C4
Poolewe 40 C1
Pooley Bridge 29 F3
Poplar 51 E3
Porlock 7 D3
Port Appin 37 D3
Port Askaig 32 B1
Port Bannatyne 33 D2
Port Driseach 33 D1
Port Ellen 32 A2
Port Erin 24 A3
Port Eynon 6 B2
Port Glasgow 33 E1
Port Henderson 40 C2
Port Logan 28 A2
Port nan Giúran 47 F2
Port nan Long 46 B1
Port Nis 47 F1
Port of Menteith 38 A4
Port St. Mary 24 A3
Port Talbot 6 C1
Port William 28 B2
Portchester 9 E3
Portencross 33 D2
Portesham 8 A4
Porth 7 D1
Porthcawl 7 D2
Porthleven 3 E4
Porthmadog 18 B3
Portishead 7 F2
Portknockie 43 D2
Portlethen 39 F1
Portmahomack 42 B1
Portnacroish 37 D2
Portnahaven 32 A2
Portnalong 40 A3
Portnancon 44 B1
Portpatrick 28 A2
Portreath 3 E3
Portree 40 B3
Portsmouth 9 E3
Portsoy 43 D2
Portway *H. & W.* 52 C4
Potten End 50 B1
Potter Street 51 F1
Potterne 8 C1
Potters Bar 16 A4
Potters Bar 50 D1
Potter's Cross 52 A3
Potters Crouch 50 C1
Potton 16 A2
Poulton-le-Fylde 24 C2
Powburn 35 F3
Powick 14 B1
Powmill 38 C4
Poyle 50 B4
Poynton 25 E4
Pratt's Bottom 51 F5
Prees 19 F3
Preesall 24 C2
Prescot 19 F1
Prestatyn 19 D1

Prestbury *Ches.* 20 B1
Prestbury *Glos.* 14 B3
Presteigne 13 F3
Preston *Dorset* 8 B4
Preston *E.Riding* 27 D3
Preston *Lancs.* 25 D3
Preston *Sc.Bord.* 35 D2
Preston Bagot 53 D5
Prestonpans 34 C1
Prestwich 25 E4
Prestwick 33 E3
Prestwick International
  Airport 33 E3
Prestwood 15 F3
Princes End 52 B2
Princes Risborough 15 E3
Princethorpe 15 D1
Princetown 4 C2
Probus 3 F3
Prudhoe 30 C2
Puddletown 8 B3
Pudsey 25 F2
Pulborough 10 A3
Pumsaint 12 C3
Purfleet 10 C1
Purfleet 51 G4
Puriton 7 F3
Purley 10 B2
Purley 51 E5
Purley on Thames 15 E4
Purton 14 C4
Putney 50 D4
Pwllheli 18 A3
Pyle 7 D2

Q

Quarry Bank 52 B3
Quedgeley 14 A3
Queenborough 11 D1
Queensbury 25 F3
Queensferry 19 E2
Queniborough 21 E3
Quernmore 25 D1
Queslett 52 C2
Quinton *W.Mid.* 52 B3

R

Rackheath 23 E3
Radcliffe *Gt.Man.* 25 E3
Radcliffe on Trent 21 E2
Radford *W.Mid.* 53 F3
Radford Semele 15 D1
Radford Semele 53 F5
Radlett 16 A4
Radlett 50 C1
Radstock 8 A1
Radford 42 B2
Raglan 7 F1
Rainford 24 C4
Rainham *Gt.Lon.* 51 G3
Rainhill 19 F1
Rainow 20 B1
Rainworth 21 E1
Rait 39 D3
Rampside 24 C1
Ramsbottom 25 E3
Ramsbury 14 C4
Ramsey *Cambs.* 16 A1
Ramsey *I.o.M.* 24 B2
Ramsey St. Mary's 22 A4
Ramsgate 11 F2
Ranskill 26 B4
Ratcliffe Culey 53 F2
Rathillet 39 D3
Ratho 34 B1

Rattray 38 C3
Raunds 15 F1
Ravenglass 29 E4
Ravenshead 21 D2
Rawcliffe *E.Riding* 26 B3
Rawcliffe *York* 26 B2
Rawmarsh 26 A4
Rawtenstall 25 E3
Rayleigh 11 D1
Rayne 16 C3
Reading 15 E4
Reay 45 D1
Red Roses 6 A1
Redbourn 16 A3
Redbridge 51 F3
Redcar 31 E3
Redcastle 41 F3
Redcliff Bay 7 F2
Redditch 14 B1
Redditch 52 C5
Redford 39 E3
Redhill *Surr.* 10 B2
Redlynch 8 C2
Rednal *W.Mid.* 52 C4
Redpoint 40 C2
Redruth 3 E3
Reepham 23 E3
Reigate 10 B2
Reiss 45 F2
Renfrew 33 F2
Rennington 35 F3
Repton 20 C3
Rescobie 39 E2
Resolven 7 D1
Reston 35 E2
Retford (East Retford)
  21 E1
Reydon 17 F1
Rhayader 13 D2
Rhiconich 44 B2
Rhondda 7 D1
Rhoose 7 E2
Rhos 6 C1
Rhos-on-Sea 18 C1
Rhoslanerchrugog 19 E2
Rhossili 6 B2
Rhu 33 E1
Rhuddlan 19 D1
Rhyl 19 D1
Rhymney 7 E1
Rhynie 43 D3
Ribchester 25 D2
Richings Park 50 B4
Richmond 30 C4
**Richmond upon Thames
  50 C4**
Rickarton 39 F1
Rickinghall 17 D1
Rickmansworth 10 A1
Rickmansworth 50 B2
Ridge *Herts.* 50 D1
Ridge Lane 53 E2
Riding Mill 30 C2
Ridley 51 H5
Rigside 34 A3
Ringford 28 C2
Ringmer 10 C4
Ringwood 8 C3
Ripley *Derbys.* 21 D2
Ripley *N.Yorks.* 26 A1
Ripon 26 A1
Ripple 14 B2
Ripponden 25 F3
Risca 7 E1
Rishton 25 D3
Risley 21 D2
Roade 15 E1

Roadside 45 E1
Roadside of Kinneff 39 F1
Roath 7 E2
Roberton *Sc.Bord.* 34 C4
Roberton *S.Lan.* 34 A3
Robin Hood's Bay 31 F4
Rocester 20 C2
Rochdale 25 E3
Roche 4 A2
Rochester *Kent* 11 D2
Rochester *Nhumb.* 35 D4
Rochford 11 D1
Rock 14 A1
Rockcliffe 29 D2
Rockingham 21 F4
Rode Heath 20 A1
Rodney Stoke 7 F3
Roehampton 50 D4
Rogart 45 D4
Rogate 9 F2
Rogerstone 7 E2
Roghad 47 D4
Romannobridge 34 B2
Romford *Gt.Lon.* 10 C1
Romford *Gt.Lon.* 51 G3
Romney Street 51 G5
Romsey 9 D2
Romsley *H. & W.* 20 B4
**Romsley *H. & W.*
  52 B3**
Ropley 9 F2
Ropsley 21 F2
Rosedale Abbey 31 E4
Rosehearty 43 F2
Rosemarkie 42 A2
Rosewell 34 B2
Roshven 37 D1
Roskhill 40 A3
Roslin 34 B2
Ross-on-Wye 14 A2
Rossett 19 E2
Rossington 26 B4
Rothbury 35 E4
Rotherfield 10 C3
Rotherham 26 A4
Rothes 42 C3
Rothesay 33 D2
Rothiesholm 49 F3
Rothley 21 E3
Rothwell *Northants.* 21 E4
Rothwell *W.Yorks.* 26 A3
Rottingdean 10 B4
Roughley 53 D2
Roughton 23 E2
Roundway 8 C1
Row Town 50 B5
Rowde 8 C1
Rowington 53 E5
Rowington Green 53 E4
Rowlands Gill 30 C2
Rowley Regis 52 B3
Rowney Green 52 C4
Roxton 16 A2
Roxwell 51 H1
Royal Leamington Spa
  14 C1
**Royal Leamington Spa
  53 F5**
Royal Tunbridge Wells
  10 C3
Roybridge 37 F1
Roydon 17 D1
Roydon Hamlet 51 F1
Royston *Herts.* 16 B2
Royston *S.Yorks.* 26 A3
Royton 25 E3
Ruabon 19 E3

Ruardean 14 A3
Rubery 52 B4
Ruddington 21 E2
Rudgwick 10 A3
Rudston 27 D1
Rufford 24 C3
Rugby 15 D1
Rugeley 20 B3
Ruislip 50 B3
Rumney 7 E2
Runcorn 19 F1
Runwell 11 D1
Rush Green 51 G3
Rushall *W.Mid.* 20 B4
Rushall *W.Mid.* 52 C1
Rushden 15 F1
Rushmere St. Andrew
  17 E2
Rushock 52 A4
Ruskington 22 A2
Ruspidge 14 A3
Rustington 10 A4
Rutherglen 33 F2
Ruthin 19 D2
Ruyton-XI-Towns 19 F3
Ryde 11 E3
Rye 11 E3
Rye Park 51 E1
Ryhall 21 F3
Ryton-on-Dunsmore 53 F4

S

Sacriston 30 C2
Saddell 32 C3
Saffron Walden 16 B2
Saham Toney 23 D4
Saighdinis 46 B1
St. Abbs 35 E1
St. Agnes 3 E3
St. Albans 16 A4
St. Albans 50 C1
St. Andrews 39 E4
St. Asaph (Llanelwy)
  19 D1
St. Athan 7 D2
St. Austell 4 A3
St. Bees 29 D3
St. Briavels 14 A2
St. Brides Major 7 D2
St. Buryan 3 D4
St. Clears 12 A4
St. Columb Major 3 F2
St. Combs 43 F2
St. Cyrus 39 F2
St. David's 12 A1
St. Day 3 E3
St. Dennis 3 F2
St. Dogmaels 12 A3
St. Endellion 4 A2
St. Enoder 3 F2
St. Fergus 43 F2
St. Fillans 38 A3
St. Germans 4 B3
St. Helens *Mersey.*
  25 D4
St. Ishmael 6 B1
St. Ive 4 B2
St. Ives *Cambs.* 16 A1
St. Ives *Cornw.* 3 D3
St. John's Chapel 30 B2
St. John's Town of Dalry
  28 C1
St. Just 3 D3
St. Just in Roseland 3 F3
St. Keverne 3 F4
St. Leonards 8 C3

St. Margaret's at Cliffe
  11 F2
St. Margaret's Hope 49 E4
St. Martin's 19 E3
St. Mary Bourne 9 D1
St. Mary Cray 51 F5
St. Mary's 49 E3
St. Mary's Bay 11 E3
St. Mawes 3 F3
St. Merryn 3 F2
St. Monans 39 E4
St. Neots 16 A1
St. Osyth 17 E3
St. Paul's Cray 51 F5
St. Peter's 11 F1
St. Stephen 3 F2
St. Stephens *Herts.* 50 C1
St. Teath 4 A2
Salcombe 4 C3
Sale 25 E4
Salen *Arg. & B.* 36 C3
Salen *High.* 37 D2
Salford *Gt.Man.* 25 E4
Salfords 10 B2
Salhouse 23 E3
Saline 34 A1
Salisbury 8 C2
Salsburgh 34 A2
Salt Hill 50 A4
Saltash 4 B2
Saltburn-by-the-Sea 31 E3
Saltcoats 33 E3
Saltdean 10 B4
Saltford 8 A1
Saltley 52 C3
Saltney 19 E2
Sanaigmore 32 A1
Sandbach 20 A1
Sanderstead 51 E5
Sandgarth 49 E3
Sandhead 28 A2
Sandhurst 9 F1
Sandiacre 21 D2
Sandness 48 A3
Sandown 9 E4
Sandplace 4 B3
Sandridge 16 A3
Sandsend 31 F3
Sandwich 11 F2
Sandwick 48 B4
Sandy 16 A2
Sandygate 24 B2
Sanquhar 34 A4
Sapcote 21 D4
Sarratt 50 B2
Sarre 11 F2
Satley 30 C2
Saundersfoot 6 A1
Sawbridgeworth 16 B3
Sawston 16 B2
Sawtry 16 A1
Saxilby 21 F1
Saxmundham 17 F1
Saxthorpe 23 E3
Scalasaig 36 B4
Scalby 31 F4
Scalloway 48 B3
Scampton 21 F1
Scapa 49 E3
Scarborough 31 F4
Scarcliffe 21 D1
Scarinish 36 A3
Scarisbrick 24 C3
Scleddau 12 B1
Scole 17 E1
Sconser 40 B3
Scorton 30 C4

Scotch Corner 30 C4
Scotter 26 C4
Scotton 30 C4
Scourie 44 A2
Scousburgh 48 B4
Scrabster 45 E1
Scraptoft 21 E3
Scremerston 35 E2
Scunthorpe 26 C3
Seaford 10 C4
Seaham 31 D2
Seahouses 35 F3
Seamer *N.Yorks.* 26 C1
Seamill 33 E2
Seascale 29 E4
Seaton *Cumb.* 29 E3
Seaton *Devon* 5 E1
Seaton Delaval 31 D1
Seaton Sluice 31 D1
Seckington 53 E1
Sedbergh 30 A4
Sedgebrook 21 F2
Sedgefield 31 D3
Sedgley 20 B4
Sedgley 52 B2
Seend 8 B1
Seer Green 50 A2
Seghill 31 D1
Seighford 20 B3
Seisdon 52 A2
Selattyn 19 E3
Selby 26 B3
Selkirk 34 C3
Sellafield 29 E4
Sellafirth 48 C1
Sellindge 11 E3
Selly Oak 52 C3
Selsdon 51 E5
Selsey 9 F4
Selston 21 D2
Send 10 A2
Sennen 3 D4
Sennybridge 13 D4
Setter 48 B3
Settle 25 E1
Seven Kings 51 F3
Seven Sisters 7 D1
Sevenoaks 10 C2
Severn Beach 7 F2
Sewardstone 51 E2
Sgiogarstaigh 47 F1
Shackerley 52 A1
Shackerstone 53 F1
Shaftesbury 8 B2
Shalfleet 9 D4
Shalford 10 A2
Shanklin 9 E4
Shap 30 A3
Shareshill 52 B1
Sharpness 14 A3
Shavington 20 A2
Shaw 25 E3
Sheepy Magna 53 F1
Sheepy Parva 53 F1
Sheering 16 B3
Sheerness 11 D1
Sheffield 26 A4
Sheffield City Airport
 26 A4
Shefford 16 A2
Sheldon *W.Mid.* 53 D3
Shelf 25 F3
Shelfield 52 C1
Shelley *Essex* 51 G1
Shellow Bowells 51 H1
Shenfield 51 H2
Shenley 50 C1

Shenleybury 50 C1
Shenstone *H. & W.* 52 A4
Shenstone *Staffs.* 20 C3
Shenstone *Staffs.* 53 D1
**Shenstone Woodend
 53 D1**
Shenton 53 F1
Shepley 25 F3
Shepperton 10 A2
Shepperton 50 B5
Shepshed 21 D3
Shepton Mallet 8 A2
Sherborne 8 A3
Sherborne St. John 9 E1
Sherburn 31 D2
Sherburn in Elmet 26 A2
Shere 10 A2
Sheriff Hutton 26 B1
Sheriffhales 20 A3
Sheringham 23 E2
Sherston 14 B4
Shevington 25 D3
Shiel Bridge 41 D4
Shieldaig 40 C2
Shifnal 20 A3
Shilbottle 35 F4
Shildon 30 C3
Shinfield 9 F1
Shinness Lodge 44 C3
Shiplake 15 E4
Shipley *Shrop.* 52 A2
Shipley *W.Yorks.* 25 F2
Shipston on Stour 14 C2
Shipton *N.Yorks.* 26 B1
Shipton *Shrop.* 20 A4
Shipton-under-Wychwood
 14 C3
Shire Oak 52 C1
Shirebrook 21 D1
Shiremoor 31 D1
Shirenewton 7 F1
Shirland 21 D1
Shirley *Gt.Lon.* 51 E5
Shirley *W.Mid.* 53 D4
Shoeburyness 11 E1
Shooter's Hill 51 F4
Shoreditch 51 E3
Shoreham *Kent* 10 C2
Shoreham *Kent* 51 H5
Shoreham-by-Sea 10 B4
Short Heath *W.Mid.* 52 C2
Shotley Gate 17 E2
Shotton *Flints.* 19 E2
Shotts 34 A2
Shrawley 52 A5
Shrewley 53 E5
Shrewsbury 13 F1
Shrewton 8 C2
Shrivenham 14 C4
Shustoke 53 E2
Shuttington 53 E1
Siabost 47 E1
Sible Hedingham 16 C2
Sibsey 22 B2
Sibson *Leics.* 53 F1
Sidbury 5 E1
Sidcup 10 C1
Sidcup 51 F4
Sidemoor 52 B4
Sidford 5 E1
Sidley 11 D1
Sidmouth 5 E1
Sigglesthorne 27 D2
Sileby 21 E3
Silloth 29 E2
Silsden 25 F2
Silverdale *Lancs.* 24 C1

Silverstone 15 E2
Silverton 5 D1
Simonsbath 6 C3
Singlewell or Ifield 51 H4
Sipson 50 B4
Sittingbourne 11 D2
Siulaisiadar 47 F2
Skaill (East Coast) *Ork.*
 49 F3
Skaill (West Coast) *Ork.*
 49 D3
Skaw 48 C2
Skegness 22 B1
Skelmersdale 24 C3
Skelmorlie 33 E2
Skelton 31 E3
Skelwick 49 E2
Skenfrith 13 F4
Skerray 44 C1
Skipness 32 C2
Skipsea 27 D2
Skipton 25 E2
Slade Green 51 G4
Slaidburn 25 D2
Slaithwaite 25 F3
Slamannan 34 A1
Sleaford 21 F2
Sledmere 26 C1
Sleights 31 F4
Sligachan 40 B3
Slinfold 10 A3
Slough 10 A1
Slough 50 A4
Smailholm 35 D3
Smalley 21 D2
Smeeth 11 E3
Smethwick 20 B4
Smethwick 52 C3
Smug Oak 50 C1
Snainton 26 C1
Snaith 26 B3
Snarestone 53 F1
Snettisham 22 C3
Snitterfield 14 C1
Snodland 11 D2
Soham 16 B1
Solas 46 B1
**Sole Street *Kent*
 51 H5**
Solihull 20 C4
Solihull 53 D4
Solihull Lodge 52 C4
Solva 12 A1
Somercotes 21 D2
Somersham 16 B1
Somerton 7 F4
Sompting 10 B4
Sonning Common 15 E4
Sorbie 28 B2
Sorisdale 36 B2
Sorn 33 F3
South Anston 26 B4
South Bank 31 E3
South Beddington 50 D5
South Benfleet 11 D1
South Brent 4 C2
South Cave 26 C3
South Chard 5 F1
South Darenth 51 G5
South Harting 9 F2
South Hetton 31 D2
South Hornchurch 51 G3
South Kelsey 27 D4
South Kirkby 26 A3
South Leverton 26 C4
South Lopham 17 D1
South Mimms 50 D1

South Molton 6 C4
South Normanton 21 D1
South Norwood 51 E5
South Ockendon 10 C1
South Ockendon 51 G3
South Oxhey 10 A1
South Oxhey 50 C2
South Petherton 7 F4
South Queensferry 34 B1
South Shields 31 D1
South Skirlaugh 27 D2
South Street *Kent* 51 H5
South Weald 51 G2
South Woodham Ferrers
 16 C4
South Wootton 22 C3
South Yardley 53 D3
Southall 50 C4
Southam 15 D1
Southampton 9 E3
Southampton International
 Airport 9 D3
Southborough 10 C3
Southbourne *W.Suss.*
 9 F3
Southdean 35 D4
Southend *Arg. & B.* 32 C4
Southend-on-Sea 11 D1
Southery 22 C4
Southfleet 51 H4
Southgate *Gt.Lon.* 10 B1
Southgate *Gt.Lon.* 50 D2
Southminster 17 D4
Southport 24 C3
Southwark 51 E4
Southwell 21 E2
Southwick *Wilts.* 8 B1
Southwold 17 F1
Sowerby 26 A1
Sowerby Bridge 25 F3
Spalding 22 A3
Spean Bridge 37 F1
Speen 9 E1
Spennymoor 31 D3
Spey Bay 42 C2
Spilsby 22 B1
Spinningdale 42 A1
Spital *Berks.* 50 A4
Spitalbrook 51 E1
Spittal 45 E2
Spittal of Glenshee 38 C2
Spixworth 23 E3
Spofforth 26 A2
Springholm 29 D1
Springside 33 E3
Sproatley 27 D2
Sprowston 23 E3
Sproxton 26 B1
Stadhampton 15 E3
Stadhlaigearraidh 46 A2
Staffin 40 B2
Stafford 20 B3
Staindrop 30 C3
Staines 10 A1
Staines 50 B4
Stainforth *N.Yorks.* 25 E1
Stainforth *S.Yorks.* 26 B3
Staintondale 31 F4
Stalbridge 8 B3
Stalham 23 F3
Stalling Busk 30 B4
Stalybridge 25 E4
Stamford 21 F3
Stamfordham 30 C1
Standeford 52 B1
Standish 25 D3

Standon 16 B3
Stane 34 A2
Stanford Rivers 51 G1
Stanford-le-Hope 11 D1
Stanhoe 22 C2
Stanhope 30 B2
Stanley *Dur.* 30 C2
Stanley *P. & K.* 38 C3
Stanley *W.Yorks.* 26 A3
Stanmore *Gt.Lon.* 50 C2
Stannington *Nhumb.*
 30 C1
Stansted 51 H5
Stansted Airport 16 B3
Stansted Mountfitchet
 16 B3
Stanton 17 D1
Stanway 17 D3
Stanwell 50 B4
Stanwell Moor 50 B4
Stapleford *Notts.* 21 D2
Stapleford Abbotts 51 F2
Stapleford Tawney 51 G2
Staplehurst 11 D2
Starcross 5 D2
Startforth 30 C3
Staunton 14 A2
Staveley 21 D1
Staxton 27 D1
Steeple Claydon 15 E2
Steeton 25 F2
Stenhousemuir 34 A1
Stenness 48 A2
Stenton 35 D1
Stepney 51 E3
Stevenage 16 A3
Stevenston 33 E3
Stewarton 33 E2
Steyning 10 B4
Stibb Cross 6 B4
Stichill 35 D3
Stickney 22 B2
Stillington *N.Yorks.* 26 B1
Stilton 22 A4
Stirchley *W.Mid.* 52 C3
Stirling 34 A1
Stivichall 53 F4
Stobo 34 B3
Stock 16 C4
Stoke Golding 53 F2
Stockingford 53 F2
Stockport 25 E4
Stocksbridge 26 A4
Stocksfield 30 C2
Stockton Heath 19 F1
Stockton-on-Tees 31 D3
Stoer 44 A3
Stoke *W.Mid.* 53 F4
Stoke Albany 21 E4
Stoke Ash 17 E1
Stoke Golding 53 F2
Stoke Holy Cross 23 E4
Stoke Mandeville 15 F3
Stoke Newington 51 E3
Stoke Poges 50 A1
Stoke Poges 50 A3
Stoke Prior *H. & W.* 14 B1
Stoke Prior *H. & W.* 52 B5
Stoke-by-Nayland 17 D2
Stoke-on-Trent 20 B2
Stokenchurch 15 E4
Stokenham 5 D3
Stokesay 13 F2
Stokesley 31 E4
Stondon Massey 51 G1
Stone *Glos.* 14 A4
Stone *H. & W.* 52 A4

tone *Kent* 10 C1
tone *Kent* 51 G4
tone *Staffs.* 20 B2
tonebridge *Warks.* 53 E3
tonehaven 39 F1
tonehouse *Glos.* 14 A3
tonehouse *S.Lan.* 34 A2
toneleigh 53 F4
toneykirk 28 A2
tonnall 52 C1
tony Stratford 15 E2
tornoway 47 F2
torrington 10 A4
totfold 16 A2
tourbridge 20 B4
tourbridge 52 A3
tourport-on-Severn 14 A1
tourport-on-Severn 52 A4
tourton *Staffs.* 52 A3
tow 34 C2
tow-on-the-Wold 14 C2
towmarket 17 D2
trachan 39 E1
trachur 37 E4
tradbroke 17 E1
tradishall 16 C2
tradsett 22 C4
traloch 38 C2
tranraer 28 A2
tratford-upon-Avon 14 C1
trathaven 33 F2
trathblane 33 F1
trathdon 42 C4
trathmiglo 38 C4
trathpeffer 41 F2
trathy 45 D1
trathyre 38 A4
tratton 4 B1
tratton St. Margaret 14 C4
treatham 50 D4
treatley 15 E4
treet 7 F4
treetly 52 C2
trensall 26 B1
tretford 25 E4
tretham 16 B1
tretton (Burton upon Trent) *Staffs.* 20 C3
trichen 43 F2
tromeferry 40 C3
tromness 49 D3
tronachlachar 37 F4
trone 33 E1
trontian 37 D2
troud 14 B3
tuartfield 43 F3
tudley *Warks.* 14 C1
tudley *Warks.* 52 C5
tudley Common 52 C5
turminster Newton 8 B3
turry 11 E2
turton le Steeple 26 C4
udbury *Derbys.* 20 C2
udbury *Gt.Lon.* 50 C3
udbury *Suff.* 17 D2
udly 7 E2
umburgh 48 A4
ummer Bridge 25 F1
unbury 10 A1
unbury 50 C5
underland 31 D2
unningdale 50 A5
unninghill 9 F1

Sunninghill 50 A5
Surbiton 50 C5
Surfleet 22 A3
Sutterton 22 A3
Sutton *Gt.Lon.* 50 D5
Sutton (Ely) *Cambs.* 16 B1
Sutton at Hone 51 H4
Sutton Bridge 22 B3
Sutton Coldfield 20 C4
Sutton Coldfield 52 D2
Sutton Courtenay 15 D4
Sutton in Ashfield 21 D1
Sutton on Trent 21 E1
Sutton Valence 11 D2
Sutton-on-the-Forest 26 B1
Swadlincote 20 C3
Swaffham 22 C4
Swanage 8 C4
Swanland 26 C3
Swanley 10 C2
Swanley 51 G5
Swanscombe 10 C1
Swanscombe 51 H4
Swansea 6 C1
Swanton Morley 23 D3
Sway 9 D3
Swindon *Glos.* 14 B2
Swindon *Staffs.* 52 A2
Swindon *Swin.* 14 C4
Swinefleet 26 C3
Swinton *Gt.Man.* 25 E4
Swinton *Sc.Bord.* 35 E2
Swinton *S.Yorks.* 26 A4
Sydenham *Gt.Lon.* 51 E4
Symbister 48 C3
Symington *S.Ayr.* 33 E3
Symington *S.Lan.* 34 A3
Synod Inn 12 B3
Syre 44 C2
Syston 21 E3
Sytchampton 52 A5

T
Tabost 47 F1
Tadcaster 26 A2
Tadley 9 E1
Taffs Well 7 E2
Tain 42 A1
Takeley 16 B3
Talgarreg 12 B3
Talgarth 13 E4
Taliesin 12 C2
Talisker 40 A3
Talladale 41 D2
Tamworth 20 C3
Tamworth 53 E1
Tannadice 39 E2
Tansley 21 D1
Tanworth in Arden 53 D4
Taobh Tuath 47 D3
Tarbert (Jura) *Arg. & B.* 32 B1
Tarbert (Kintyre) *Arg. & B.* 32 C2
Tarbet 37 F4
Tarbolton 33 F3
Tardebigge 52 B5
Tarfside 39 E1
Tarleton 24 C3
Tarporley 19 F2
Tarrel 42 B1
Tarves 43 E3
Tarvin 19 F2
Tattershall 22 A2
Taunton 7 E4

Taverham 23 E3
Tavistock 4 C2
Tayinloan 32 C2
Taynuilt 37 E3
Tayport 39 D3
Tayvallich 32 C1
Teangue 40 C4
Tebay 30 A4
Teddington *Gt.Lon.* 50 C4
Tees-side Airport 31 D3
Teignmouth 5 D2
Telford 20 A3
Temple Bar 12 B3
Temple Sowerby 30 A3
Templeton 6 A1
Tenbury Wells 14 A1
Tenby 6 A1
Tenterden 11 D3
Terrington 26 B1
Terrington St. Clement 22 B3
Tetbury 14 B4
Tetford 22 A1
Tetney 27 E4
Tettenhall 52 A1
Tettenhall Wood 52 A2
Teviothead 34 C4
Tewkesbury 14 B2
Teynham 11 E2
Thame 15 E3
Thames Ditton 50 C5
Thamesmead 51 F3
Thatcham 9 E1
Thaxted 16 C2
The Bratch 52 A2
The Burf 52 A5
The Mumbles 6 C2
The Stocks 11 D3
The Wrythe 50 D5
Theale 15 E4
Thetford 23 D4
Theydon Bois 51 F2
Thirsk 26 A1
Thong 51 H4
Thornaby-on-Tees 31 D3
Thornbury 14 A4
Thorne 26 B3
Thornes 52 C1
Thorney *Bucks.* 50 B4
Thorney *Cambs.* 22 A4
Thorngumbald 27 D3
Thornhill *D. & G.* 34 A4
Thornhill *Stir.* 38 A4
Thornley 31 D2
Thornton *Fife* 39 D4
Thornton *Lancs.* 24 C2
Thornton *Mersey.* 24 C4
Thornton Dale 26 C1
Thornwood Common 51 F1
Thorpe *Surr.* 50 B5
Thorpe Constantine 53 E1
Thorpe Market 23 E2
Thorpe on the Hill *Lincs.* 21 F1
Thorpe St. Andrew 23 E4
Thorpe-le-Soken 17 E3
Thorpeness 17 F1
Thrapston 21 F4
Threlkeld 29 F3
Threshers Bush 51 F1
Threshfield 25 E1
Thropton 35 E4
Thrumster 45 F2
Thrupp 14 B3
Thrybergh 26 A4
Thundersley 11 D1
Thurcroft 26 A4

Thurlby 22 A3
Thurmaston 21 E3
Thurnscoe 26 A4
Thursby 29 F2
Thurso 45 E1
Thurton 23 E4
Thwaite 30 B4
Tibbermore 38 C3
Tibshelf 21 D1
Ticehurst 11 D3
Tickhill 26 B4
Ticknall 21 D3
Tidenham 14 A4
Tideswell 20 C1
Tighnabruaich 33 D1
Tilbury 10 C1
Tilbury 51 H4
Tile Cross 53 D3
Tile Hill 53 E4
Tilehurst 15 E4
Tillicoultry 38 B4
Tillyfourie 43 D4
Tilston 19 F2
Timsbury 8 A1
Timsgearraidh 47 D2
Tingewick 15 E2
Tingwall 49 E3
Tintagel 4 A1
Tintern Parva 7 F1
Tipton 52 B2
Tiptree 17 D3
Tisbury 8 B2
Tiverton 7 D4
Toab 48 B4
Tobermory 36 C2
Toberonochy 37 D4
Toddington *Beds.* 15 F2
Toddington *Glos.* 14 B2
Todmorden 25 E3
Toft 48 B2
Togston 35 F4
Tolastadh a'Chaolais 47 E2
Tolastadh Ur 47 F1
Toll of Birness 43 F3
Tollesbury 17 D3
Tolleshunt D'Arcy 17 D3
Tolworth 50 C5
Tomatin 42 A3
Tomich 42 A2
Tomintoul 42 C4
Tomnavoulin 42 C3
Tonbridge 10 C2
Tongland 28 C2
Tongue 44 C1
Tonna 6 C1
Tonypandy 7 D1
Tonyrefail 7 D2
Toot Hill 51 G1
Topcliffe 26 A1
Topsham 5 D1
Tore 41 F2
Tormore 32 C3
Torphichen 34 A1
Torphins 43 D4
Torpoint 4 B3
Torquay 5 D2
Torrance 33 F1
Torridon 41 D2
Torrin 40 B4
Torthorwald 29 E1
Torver 29 F4
Toscaig 40 C3
Tosside 25 E2
Totland 9 D4
Totnes 5 D2
Tottenham 51 E2

Totteridge 50 D2
Tottington 25 E3
Totton 9 D3
Tow Law 30 C2
Towcester 15 E2
Tower Hamlets 51 E3
Town Yetholm 35 E3
Townhead of Greenlaw 29 D1
Towyn 19 D1
Tranent 34 C1
Trawsfynydd 18 C3
Trecastle 13 D4
Tredegar 7 E1
Tredington 14 C2
Treeton 26 A4
Trefaldwyn (Montgomery) 13 E1
Trefeglwys 13 D2
Trefriw 18 C2
Trefnwy (Monmouth) 7 F1
Tregaron 12 C3
Tregony 3 F3
Tregynon 13 E1
Treharris 7 E1
Treherbert 7 D1
Trelech 12 A4
Trelleck 7 F1
Tremadog 18 B3
Trenance 3 F2
Trescott 52 A2
Tressait 38 B2
Tretower 13 E4
Trimdon 31 D3
Trimsaran 6 B1
Tring 15 F3
Trinity 39 E2
Trochry 38 C3
Troedyrhiw 7 E1
Troon 33 E3
Troutbeck 29 F4
Troutbeck Bridge 29 F4
Trowbridge 8 B1
Trumpington 16 B2
Truro 3 F3
Trysull 52 A2
Tudweiliog 18 A3
Tummel Bridge 38 B2
Tunga 47 F2
Tunstall *Suff.* 17 F2
Turnberry 33 E4
Turner's Green 53 D4
Turners Hill 10 B3
Turnford 51 E1
Turriff 43 E2
Tutbury 20 C3
Tutnall 52 B4
Tutshill 7 F1
Tuxford 21 E1
Twatt 49 D3
Twechar 33 F1
Tweedmouth 35 E2
Tweedsmuir 34 B3
Twickenham 50 C4
Two Gates 53 E1
Twycross 53 F1
Twyford *Berks.* 15 E4
Twyford *Hants.* 9 E2
Twynholm 28 C2
Twyning 14 B2
Tyburn 53 D2
Tye Common 51 H2
Tylers Green *Essex* 51 G1
Tyndrum 37 F3
Tynemouth 31 D1
Tythegston 7 D2

Winsford *Ches.* 19 F2
Winsley 8 B1
Winslow 15 E2
Winston 30 C3
Winterbourne 14 A4
Winterbourne Abbas 8 A4
Winterton 26 C3
Winton 30 B3
Winwick *Cambs.* 16 A1
Wirksworth 20 C2
Wisbech 22 B3
Wishaw *N.Lan.* 34 A2
Wishaw *Warks.* 53 D2
Wistanstow 13 F2
Wistaston 20 A2
Witham 16 C3
Witheridge 7 D4
Witherley 53 F2
Withernsea 27 E3
Witley 9 F2
Witney 15 D3
Wittering 21 F3
Witton Gilbert 30 C2
Wiveliscombe 7 E4
Wivenhoe 17 D3
Woburn 15 F2
Woburn Sands 15 F2
Woking 10 A2
Wokingham 9 F1
Wold Newton 27 D1
Wollaston *Northants.*
    15 F1

Wollaston *W.Mid.* 52 A3
Wolsingham 30 C2
Wolston 15 D1
Wolverhampton 20 B4
Wolverhampton 52 B2
Wolverley *H. & W.*
    20 B4
**Wolverley *H. & W.*
    52 A4**
Wolverton *M.K.* 15 E2
Wolverton *Warks.* 53 E5
Wombourne 20 B4
Wombourne 52 A2
Wombwell 26 A4
Wooburn 10 A1
**Wood End (Redditch)
    Warks. 53 D4**
**Wood End (Tamworth)
    Warks. 53 E2**
Wood Green 51 E2
Wood Hayes 52 B1
Woodborough 21 E2
Woodbridge 17 E2
Woodcote 15 E4
Woodford *Gt.Lon.* 51 F2
Woodford Bridge 51 F2
Woodford Green 51 F2
**Woodgate *H. & W.*
    52 B5**
**Woodgate *W.Mid.*
    52 B3**
Woodhall Spa 22 A1

Woodham *Surr.* 50 B5
Woodingdean 10 B4
Woodland 30 C3
Woodley 15 E4
Woodmansey 27 D2
Woodplumpton 25 D2
Woodside *Berks.* 50 A4
Woodside *Herts.* 50 D1
Woodside *W.Mid.* 52 B3
Woodstock 15 D3
Woodton 23 E4
Woodville 20 C3
Wool 8 B4
Woolacombe 6 B3
Wooler 35 E3
Woolmere Green 52 B5
Woolston *Ches.* 19 F1
Woolwich 51 F4
Wootton 15 F2
Wootton Bassett 14 C4
Wootton Wawen 53 D5
Worcester 14 B1
Worcester Park 50 D5
Wordsley 52 A3
Worfield 20 A4
Workington 29 E3
Worksop 21 E1
Wormit 39 D3
Wormley *Herts.* 51 E1
Worplesdon 10 A2
Worth 10 B3
Worthing 10 A4

Wotton-under-Edge 14 A4
Woughton on the Green
    15 F2
Wragby 22 A1
Wrangle 22 B2
Wraysbury 50 B4
Wrea Green 24 C3
Wrelton 31 F4
Wrexham 19 E2
Wrington 7 F2
Writtle 16 C4
Wrotham Hill 51 H5
Wrotham Park 50 D2
Wroughton 14 C4
Wroxhall 53 E4
Wyberton 22 A2
Wychbold 52 B5
Wye 11 E2
Wylde Green 53 D2
Wylye 8 C2
Wymondham *Leics.* 21 F3
Wymondham *Norf.* 23 E4
Wyre Piddle 14 B2
Wythall 14 C1
Wythall 52 C4

Y

Y Drenewydd (Newtown)
    Powys 13 E2
Yapton 10 A4
Yardley 53 D3

Yarm 31 D3
Yarmouth 9 D4
Yarnton 15 D3
Yarrow 34 C3
Yate 14 A4
Yateley 9 F1
Yatton 7 F2
Yaxley 22 A4
Yeading 50 C3
Yeadon 25 F2
Yealmpton 4 C3
Yeovil 7 F4
Yeovilton 7 F4
Yetts o' Muckhart 38 C4
Yiewsley 50 B4
Ynysddu 7 E1
York 26 B2
Youlgreave 20 C1
Yoxall 20 C3
Yoxford 17 F1
Ysbyty Ystwyth 12 C2
Ystalyfera 6 C1
Ystrad 7 D1
Ystradgynlais 6 C1

Z

Zennor 3 D3

INDEX TO PLACE NAMES OF IRELAND

Abbreviations

Ant. County Antrim	*Kerry* County Kerry	*Meath* County Meath	*Water.* County Waterford
Down County Down	*Kilk.* County Kilkenny	*Tipp.* County Tipperary	*Wexf.* County Wexford
Dub. County Dublin	*Mayo* County Mayo	*Tyr.* County Tyrone	

Aasleagh 56 B3
Abbeyfeale 58 C2
Abbeyleix 60 A3
Achill 56 B2
Adare 58 C1
Annahilt 55 E3
Annalong 55 F4
Antrim 55 E2
Ardara 54 B2
Ardee 55 E4
Ardglass 55 F3
Arklow (An tinbhear Mór) 60 B3
Armagh 55 E3
Armoy 55 E1
Arvagh 57 E2
Ashbourne 60 B1
Athboy 57 F3
Athenry 57 D4
Athleague 57 D3
Athlone (Baile Átha Luain) 57 E3
Athy 57 F4
Augher 55 D3
Aughnacloy 55 D3
Aughrim 60 B3
Avoca 60 B3

B

Baillieborough 57 F2
Balbriggan 60 B1
Ballaghaderreen 57 D2
Ballina 56 C2
Ballinafad 57 D2
Ballinalack 57 E3
Ballinamore 57 E2
Ballinasloe (Béal Átha na Sluaighe) 57 D4
Ballindine 56 C3
Ballinrobe 56 C3
Ballon 60 A3
Ballybay 57 F2
Ballybofey 54 C2
Ballybrack 58 A3
Ballybunnion 58 B2
Ballycanew 60 B3
Ballycastle *Ant.* 55 E1
Ballycastle *Mayo* 54 A3
Ballyclare 55 E2
Ballyconnell 57 E2
Ballycroy 56 B2
Ballydesmond 58 C2
Ballygar 57 D3
Ballygawley 55 D3
Ballygorman 55 D1
Ballyhale 60 A4
Ballyhaunis 57 D3
Ballyheige 58 B2
Ballyjamesduff 57 F2
Ballylynan 60 A3
Ballymacarberry 59 E2
Ballymacmague 59 E3
Ballymacoda 59 E3
Ballymahon 57 E3
Ballymakeery 58 C3

Ballymena 55 E2
Ballymoney 55 E2
Ballymote 57 D2
Ballymurphy 60 A3
Ballynahinch 55 F3
Ballyragget 60 A3
Ballyshannon 54 B3
Ballyvaughan 56 C4
Ballyward 55 E3
Baltinglass 60 B3
Banagher 57 E4
Banbridge 55 E3
Bandon 59 D3
Bangor 56 B2
Bangor Erris 56 F3
Banteer 58 C2
Bantry 58 B4
Belcoo 54 C3
Belderg 56 B1
Belfast 55 F3
Belfast International Airport 55 E3
Belmullet 56 B2
Beragh 55 D3
Bessbrook 55 E4
Bettystown 60 B1
Birr 57 E4
Blackrock 55 E4
Blackwater 60 B4
Blarney 59 D3
Blessington 60 B2
Bohola 56 C2
Borris 60 A3
Borrisokane 57 D4
Borrisoleigh 59 E1
Boyle 57 D2
Bray (Bré) 60 B2
Broadford 58 C2
Broughshane 55 E2
Bunbeg 54 B2
Bunclody 60 B3
Buncrana 54 C1
Bundoran 54 B3
Burtonport 54 B2
Bushmills 55 E1
Butlers Bridge 57 F2
Buttevant 59 D2

C

Cahermore 58 B4
Cahir 59 E2
Cahirciveen 58 A3
Callan 60 A4
Cappoquin 59 E2
Carlingford 55 E4
Carlow (Ceatharlach) 60 A3
Carndonagh 55 D1
Carnlough 55 E2
Carrick-on-Shannon 57 E2
Carrick-on-Suir (Carraig na Sivire) 60 A4
Carrickfergus 55 F2
Carrickmacross 57 F2
Carrigallen 57 E2

Carrigtwohill 59 D3
Carrowdore 55 F3
Carrowkeel 55 D1
Cashel 59 E2
Castlebar (Caisleán an Bharraigh) 56 C2
Castlebellingham 55 E4
Castleblayney 57 F2
Castlebridge 60 B4
Castlecomer 60 A3
Castleconnell 59 D1
Castlederg 54 C2
Castledermot 60 A3
Castlegregory 58 B2
Castleisland 58 B2
Castlemaine 58 B2
Castlemartyr 59 E3
Castlepollard 57 F3
Castlerea 57 D3
Castletown 57 E4
Castletown Bere 58 B4
Catherdaniel 58 A3
Cavan 57 F2
Celbridge 60 B2
Charlestown 57 D2
Cheekpoint 60 A4
City of Derry Airport 55 D2
Clady 54 C2
Clane 60 B2
Clara 57 E4
Clarecastle 58 C1
Claregatway 56 C4
Claremorris 56 C3
Clashmore 59 E3
Claudy 55 D2
Clifden 56 B3
Cliffonoy 54 B3
Cloghan 57 E4
Clogheen 59 E2
Clonakilty 58 C4
Clonbern 57 D3
Clones 57 F2
Clonmel (Cluain Meala) 59 E2
Clonroche 60 B4
Clonygowan 57 F4
Cloonbannin 58 C2
Clooneagh 57 E2
Cobh (An Cóbh) 59 D3
Coleraine 55 D1
Collooney 57 D2
Comber 55 F3
Cong 56 C3
Cookstown 55 D3
Cootehill 57 F2
Cork (Corcaigh) 59 D3
Cork Airport 59 D3
Corofin 58 C1
Courtmacsherry 59 D4
Courtown 60 B3
Craanford 60 B3
Craigavon 55 E3
Creeslough 54 C1
Cregganbaun 56 B3
Crookhaven 58 B4

Croom 59 D2
Crossgar 55 F3
Crosshaven 59 D3
Crossmaglen 55 E4
Crumlin 55 E3
Crusheen 58 C1
Cullybackey 55 E2
Cushendall 55 E2
Cushendun 55 E1

D

Delvin 57 F3
Dingle 58 A2
Donaghadee 55 F3
Donegal 54 B3
Dooagh 56 B2
Downpatrick 55 F3
Draperstown 55 D2
Drimoleague 58 C4
Drogheda (Droichead Átha) 60 B1
Dromod 57 E2
Dromore *Down* 55 E3
Dromore *Tyr.* 54 C3
Dromore West 56 C2
Drumfree 54 C1
Drumkeeran 57 D2
Drummin 60 A4
Dublin (Baile Átha Cliath) 60 B2
Dublin Airport 60 B1
Dunboyne 60 B1
Duncannon 60 A4
Duncormick 60 B4
Dundalk (Dún Dealgan) 55 E4
Dundonald 55 F3
Dundrum 55 F3
Dungannon 55 D3
Dungarvan *Kilk.* 60 A3
Dungarvan *Water.* 59 E3
Dungiven 55 D2
Dungloe 54 B2
Dunlavin 60 B2
Dunleer 55 E4
Dunloy 55 E2
Dunmanway 58 C3
Dunmore 57 D3
Dunmore East 60 A4
Dunmurry 55 E3
Dunquin 58 A2
Durrow 60 A3
Dún Laoghaire 60 B2

E

Edenderry 57 F4
Edgeworthstown 57 E3
Eglinton 55 D2
Ennis (Inis) 58 C1
Enniscorthy (Inis Córthaidh) 60 B4
Enniskean 58 C3
Enniskerry 60 B2

Enniskillen 54 C3
Ennistymon 58 C1

F

Fermoy 59 D2
Ferns 60 B3
Fethard 59 E2
Fintona 55 D3
Fintown 54 B2
Fivemiletown 55 D3
Foxford 56 C2
Foynes 58 C1
Frenchpark 57 D2
Freshford 60 A3

G

Galbally 59 D2
Galway (Gaillimh) 56 C4
Garvagh 55 D2
Glenamaddy 57 D3
Glengarriff 58 B3
Glengavlen 57 E2
Glenties 54 B2
Gorey 60 B3
Gort 56 C4
Gortahork 54 B1
Graigue 60 A3
Graiguenamanagh 60 A3
Granard 57 E3
Grange 59 E3
Greenore 55 E4
Gweedore 54 B2

H

Halfway 59 D3
Headford 56 C3
Holycross 59 E1
Horseleap 57 D3
Hospital 59 D2
Howth 60 B1
Hurler's Cross 58 C1

I

Inch *Kerry* 58 B2
Inch *Wexf.* 60 B3

J

Johnstown 59 E1

K

Kanturk 58 C2
Keady 55 D4
Kells *Kilk.* 60 A4
Kells (Ceanannus Mór) *Meath* 57 F3
Kenmare 58 B3
Kilbeggan 57 E4
Kilcolgan 56 C4

ilcommon 59 E2
ilcoole 60 B2
ilcormac 57 E4
ilcullen 57 F4
ildare 57 F4
ilkee 58 B1
ilkeel 55 E4
ilkenny (Cill Chainnigh)
  60 A3
illala 56 C2
illaloe 59 D1
illarney (Cill Airne)
  58 B3
illenaule 59 E1
illimor 57 D4
illinchy
illinick 60 B4
illorglin 58 B3
illurin 60 B4
illybegs 54 B3
ilmacrenan 54 C2
ilmaine 56 C3
ilmallock 59 D2
ilmona 59 D3
ilmore Quay 60 B4
ilrea 55 E2
ilrush 58 B1
ilteel 60 B2
iltimagh 56 C2
itullagh 57 D4
ingscourt 57 F2
innegad 57 F3
insale 59 D3
invara 56 C4
irkcubbin 55 F3
nock 56 C3
nock Airport
  56 C3
nockalough 58 C1
nocktopher 60 A4

anesborough
  57 E3
arne 55 F2
auragh 58 B3
eap 58 C4
eighlinbridge 60 A3
eixlip 60 B2
etterkenny 54 C2
fford 54 C2
mavady 55 D2

Limerick (Luimneach)
  59 D1
Lisbellaw 54 C3
Lisburn 55 E3
Lisdoonvarna 56 C4
Lismore 59 E2
Lisnarrick 54 C3
Lisnaskea 54 C4
Listowel 58 B2
Londonderry (Derry)
  55 D2
Longford 57 E3
Loughrea 57 D4
Louisburgh 56 B3
Lucan 60 B2
Lukeswell 60 A4
Lurgan 55 E3

M
Macroom 58 C3
Maghera 55 E2
Magherafelt 55 E2
Malahide 60 B1
Malin More 54 B2
Mallow (Mala) 59 D2
Manorhamilton 54 B3
Markethill 55 E3
May's Corner 55 E3
Middletown 55 D3
Midleton 59 D3
Milestone 59 E1
Milford 54 C2
Millstreet 58 C3
Milltown Malbay
  58 C1
Mitchelstown 59 D2
Moate 57 E4
Mohill 57 E2
Moira 55 E3
Monaghan (Muineachán)
  57 F2
Monasterevan 57 F4
Moneygall 59 E1
Moneymore 55 E2
Monivea 57 D4
Mount Bellew 57 D3
Mountmellick 57 F4
Mountrath 57 E4
Mountshannon 59 D1
Moville 55 D1
Moyvalley 57 F3
Muine Bheag 60 A3

Mullany's Cross 56 C2
Mullingar (Án Muileann
  gCearr) 57 F3
Mulrany 56 B2
Murroogh 56 C4

N
Naas (An Nás) 60 B2
Navan (An Uaimh) 60 B1
Nenagh (An tAonach)
  59 D1
New Ross 60 A4
Newbridge 57 F4
Newcastle *Down* 55 F4
Newcastle *Dub.* 55 F4
Newcastle West 58 C2
Newinn 59 E2
Newmarket 58 C2
Newmarket-on-Fergus
  58 C1
Newport *Mayo* 56 B2
Newport *Tipp.* 59 D1
Newry 55 E4
Newtown 59 D2
Newtownabbey 55 F3
Newtownards 55 F3
Newtownbutler 57 F2
Newtownmountkennedy
  60 B2
Newtownstewart 55 D2
Ninemilehouse 59 E2
Nobber 55 D4

O
Oldcastle 57 F3
Omagh 55 D3
Oranmore 56 C4

P
Pallas Green 59 D1
Park 55 D2
Partry 56 C3
Pettigo 54 C3
Pomeroy 55 D3
Pontoon 56 C2
Portadown 55 E3
Portaferry 55 F3
Portarlington 57 F4
Portavogie 55 F3
Portlaoise 57 F4

Portlaw 60 A4
Portmagee 58 A3
Portrane 60 B1
Portrush 55 E1
Portsalon 54 C1
Portstewart 55 D1
Portumna 57 D4
Poulgorm Bridge 58 C3

R
Randalstown 55 E2
Raphoe 54 C2
Rathangan 54 F4
Rathdowney 59 E1
Rathdrum 60 B3
Rathfriland 55 E4
Rathkeale 58 C2
Rathkeevin 59 E2
Rathluirc (Charleville)
  59 D2
Rathvilly 60 B3
Recess 56 B3
Ringsend 55 D2
Roscommon 57 D3
Roscrea 59 E1
Ross Carbery 58 C4
Rosslare 60 B4
Rosslare Harbour 60 B4
Rosslea 55 D4
Rush 60 B1

S
Saintfield 55 F3
Schull 58 B4
Shanacrane 58 C3
Shannon Airport 58 C1
Shercock 57 F2
Shillelagh 60 B3
Sion Mills 54 C2
Sixmilebridge 59 D1
Skerries 60 B1
Skibbereen 58 C4
Slane 60 B1
Sligo (Sligeach) 54 B3
Sneem 58 B3
Strabane 54 C2
Stradbally 57 F4
Strangford 55 F3
Stranorlar 54 C2
Strokestown 57 D3
Swinford 56 C2

Swords 60 B1

T
Taghmon 60 B4
Tallow 59 E3
Tandragee 55 E3
Tarbert 58 C1
Templemore 59 E1
Templetuohy 59 E1
Thomastown 60 A4
Thurles (Durlas) 59 E1
Timolin 57 F4
Tipperary 59 D2
Tower 59 D3
Tralee (Trá Lí) 58 B2
Tramore (Trá Mhór)
  60 A4
Trim 57 F3
Tuam 56 C3
Tubbercurry 57 D2
Tulla 59 D1
Tullamore (Tulach Mhór)
  57 E4
Tullow 60 A3
Tully 54 C3
Tulsk 57 D3

U
Urlingford 59 E1

V
Virginia 57 F2

W
Warrenpoint 55 E4
Waterford (Port Láirgé)
  60 A4
Watergrasshill 59 D3
Wellington Bridge
  60 A4
Westport 56 B3
Wexford (Loch Garman)
  60 B4
Whitehall 60 A3
Whitehead 55 F2
Wicklow 60 C2

Y
Youghal (Eochaill) 59 E3